PLUNGE

Midlife with Snorkel

MARI ANDERSON & FRITZ DAMLER

Tinkertown Press ISBN-13   978-0-9793124-3-4

Cover photo and design by Mari Anderson
Author photo by Christopher Dempsey
Interior photos by Mari Anderson & Fritz Damler unless otherwise noted

www.plungethebook.com

For Margaret June Olson, Walter (Fred) Damler,
Elizabeth Marietta, James Guthro,
and Esmeralda

We miss you.

Acknowledgments

This is a story about our first four years of building a home on Crooked Island, Bahamas. To anyone we misquoted, misrepresented or forgot, we apologize. (You know there's a good chance we didn't do it on purpose.)

We thank:

~ The people of Crooked Island, Bahamas, for your graciousness and your open hearts.

~ All our friends and family members who have visited, written, commiserated and understood that life off the beaten path is rarely easy, profitable or predictable. And that is the point.

Contents

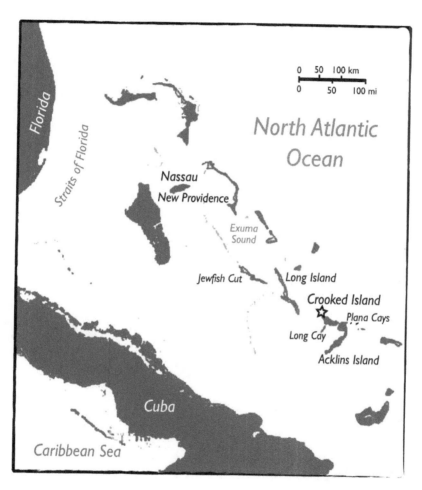

The Bahamas

Prologue
Ready, Set...

Mari:

It was Monday, 5 a.m. I'd been up all night stewing about a mistake I made in an ad for a big client. An ad that right then was being distributed all over the county as part of the current year's New Mexico Vacation Guide. It was two full pages. Color. Gorgeous photos, clever copy. And the wrong toll-free number. Instead of linking callers to the right office, the phone was answered by a thick-accented man in an off-track betting lounge in New York City. He was not the least bit interested in giving up his phone number to solve my problem.

How could this have happened? So many eyes had proofread so many versions of the ad we must have become blind to the disaster that stared at us from the middle of the page. My client was understanding and gracious, but ultimately the responsibility for the goof was mine, all mine. After 24 hours of brooding I still felt like throwing up, but finally managed to nod off to sleep. That's when the phone rang.

A client who was in Boston for a conference needed to catch me, she said, before heading into all-day meetings. She was sorry to call so early, but simply had to make a change in her business brochure. A brochure that I'd delivered to the printer two days before.

As the sky started to lighten, I started the coffee maker and sifted through the previous day's mail, forcing myself to open an envelope with *Taxation and Revenue Department* as the return address. The prior year, to nudge my little business towards more financial professionalism, I'd hired a zippy new tax guy, so this shouldn't be scary. But this letter informed me my previous year's gross receipts reports didn't match the amount reported on my federal income tax. That's a big no-no. I'd not been charging tax to some clients who represented themselves as non-profit. Non-profit they may have been but without, it turns out, the requisite, official, designation. Now I'd have to go back and collect all those taxes or pay them myself, plus a hefty fine.

It was Monday, 5:30 a.m. I wasn't so tired, frustrated or stressed that I couldn't find my way through it all. But at that moment I started to wonder about my life, and about the box I'd created for myself. I started to think about how lovely but foreign the word *spacious* had begun to sound.

Fritz:

There is an old Cole Porter song that goes: *Oh give me land, lots of land, with starry skies above. Don't fence me in...* It was my theme song. After ten years at sea on a 35-foot wooden sailboat, followed by five years managing a retreat center in the mountains of New Mexico, Albuquerque's North Valley seemed pretty urban to me. Deep down I could feel the 24/7 hum of the city. I missed the quiet. I'd barricaded myself on our half acre of land. Home Depot and Barnes and Noble were within walking distance. The thought of driving across town to see a movie, eat at a restaurant, or attend a concert gave me the chills. I even found a Tae Kwon Do studio that I could get to, avoiding all but two traffic lights.

Between a bit of day trading in that crazy dot-com era and working on my third novel, I rarely had to leave the house. All my visions of paradise had those starry skies and uninterrupted vistas, be they land or sea. What would it take to change the picture? Certainly an opportunity if we recognized it as such, and of course, some money. Our finances were primarily tied up in the house, the remnants of my rug business and Mari's graphic design company. It's not like we had vast resources or big savings accounts.

But the question always remains, how thin does the ice have to get before you stop walking? Until it starts to crack? I knew I was ready to keep moving forward, and I didn't mind the thought of getting wet.

Mari/Fritz:

Talk to almost anyone, especially those of us at midlife (handy euphemism for the stage of life just prior to "old") and they will tell you of a moment, or a period of time in their lives when they could have made a radical change. And didn't. Of course, like beauty or fear, the concept of "radical change" is in the eye and emotions of the beholder. For us it might be staying home on New Year's Eve instead of going out. For you it's divorce, Peace Corps, teaching yoga in Africa.

The same goes for paradise. We say sandy beach/palm trees/salt water; you say chateau/vineyard/1-speed bicycle. (Actually, we have lots of versions of paradise and you probably do, too, depending on the season, your mood, even the day of the week.)

But even though our notions of the perfect place to be and to live may change through the years, the way to reach Nirvana never does. There's always that moment, a jumping-off point, the words, *why not?* Followed by a plunge.

This is the story of ours.

Armando's Flight

(When you see this fish it's Mari talking)

Today an elfin, curly-haired Venezuelan man dropped from the sky. A violent thunderstorm had just swept through; our aluminum shutters still pinged with the last remnants of hard, horizontal rain. The sharp smell of ozone permeated the rock walls of the house. A high-pitched buzz, distinctly different than the one small airplanes make when landing, replaced the sound of rain. Fritz looked outside just as the contraption responsible vanished beneath the line of coconut palms.

"What the devil was that?" he said. "Let's go check it out."

We quickly drove the half-mile to the landing strip. Sitting there was a tiny, torpedo-nosed bumper-car on three wheels topped with a tent pole-like framework that supported a single, triangular wing. What looked like a large lunch box covered with wires was suspended behind the seat. Attached to the lunch box, a red-tipped propeller. If Mary Poppins had decided to upgrade her umbrella, she might have gone for this machine.

It had already attracted a crowd. The pilot, who emerged smiling from the middle, looked more like Frodo the Hobbit than a prim English nanny. And like Frodo, he was on a quest.

"Armando," he said, and shook hands all around.

He'd left Orlando two days before, intending to island-hop to Caracas, Venezuela, in time for the 100-year anniversary of flight on December 17, 2004. There was going to be a big party, he told us. If he made it, his flight would earn him a mention in the Guinness Book of World Records. This meant Armando from Orlando still had over fifteen hundred miles to travel. In six days.

The original aft seat of his motorized hang-glider had been replaced by a 26-gallon fuel tank, enough for about four hours of flight. The wingspan was short by comparison to most ultra-lights; Armando's priority was speed, not glide. To make up for it he flew high. If his engine quit between 5,000 and 10,000 feet, he'd have nearly forty miles of glide time to spot an island or cay (key) for emergency landing. His little air machine had no floats; water landing was not an option.

Armando quickly began to peel off three pairs of pants, a turtleneck, two sweaters, fleece pullover and leather jacket. "It is bery, bery cold up there," he said, already sweating. It was currently 78° on the ground.

Crooked Island, Bahamas, had not been on his original itinerary but the squall with "rain like needles" forced him to descend until the storm passed. The storm was headed the same direction he was, towards the Turks and Caicos Islands. With the existing tailwind, he expected to fly at up to ninety miles per hour, easily overtaking the same conditions he'd just escaped. Already feeling deputized as ground crew in Armando's quirky campaign, Fritz and I invited him to lunch. We also offered our guest room in case he was grounded overnight.

The 1 p.m. weather report on ZNS radio predicted a cold front headed our way from the northern Bahamas. If it cleared to the south, Armando said he might chance an afternoon flight to the Turks and Caicos, or at least Mayaguana, which was a hundred miles southeast.

While we ate, we learned more about our unexpected guest. This was no boy on a coming-of-age joyride. In 1995, Armando, his wife and two children had left Venezuela for the safety of the States after two incidents. His teenaged daughter had been robbed as she left a bank in Caracas. Months later, two bullets struck his wife's car as she sped away from attempted hijackers.

Their transition was eased by Armando's dual citizenship; his father was Venezuelan, his mother American. In Orlando, he'd found work at Disney World, spending his days underwater feeding fish in the sea exhibit. He said he felt lucky to have the job. "I am scuba diver. Who could think I'd get paid to do what I love?"

By the time we finished lunch, the sky looked clear in all directions. Armando called home and left the message that he was safe and once again on his way. He also left our phone number so his wife could call us back later for details.

We drove him to the landing strip and he began to layer on all his clothing. Before the heat made him light-headed, Armando hurried through his pre-flight check while Fritz and neighbor Jim Finley released the glider's tie-down straps. Then, handshakes. Hugs. Photos and thank-you's. A promise extracted to not allow his desire for success compromise his good judgment. Another promise to call when he reached, or did not reach, his destination.

Then he pulled the crank, the engine caught, the prop whirled. He strapped himself in and taxied down the runway. When he reached the far end he pivoted, then sped past us, lifted and waved. He arced a half-circle over casuarina pines and was gone.

Fritz and I listened as the sound of the engine grew faint. The pines still radiated a shimmer of color, like the afterglow of sunset. We drove home smiling and silent.

Six days passed. We spoke of Armando every day, guessing where he might be. From the Turks and Caicos he'd planned to stop in Puerto Plata, the Dominican Republic, then Puerto Rico and south to the Leeward, then Windward Islands: St. Croix, Saba, Nevis, St. Kitts, Montserrat, Guadeloupe, St. Lucia, St. Vincent and finally, the coast of Venezuela and home. A friend had set up a website to track his progress, but we had no way to access it.

On the evening of Wednesday the 17th, his targeted date of arrival, we decided to call his wife. Before we could dial, the phone rang. Fritz answered, and after a moment said, "Armando! Que Pasa?" Then, "At least you're safe."

He was in an airport en route to Miami, then home. As he'd left Puerto Rico his engine had begun to repeatedly stall. Even though he'd been able to restart it each time, he knew it was too dangerous to continue. True to his promise to put his safety first, he returned to Puerto Rico and caught a commercial flight home. In January he'd try again, he told Fritz, who asked him to stop again on Crooked, this time on purpose. He promised he would.

Armando's flight felt like one of those oddly wonderful events that sometimes slip through the normal matrix of time and experience. Since building a home on Crooked Island five years before, I'd almost come to expect them. Whether it was the island itself or the decision to leave urban life, career and the expectations that accompanied them, it seemed we'd put ourselves on the path of wonder.

It was inexplicable, really, why someone with a family, a home and a job would fly a machine that looked like a cereal-box prize at 10,000 feet wearing a closet-full of winter clothes. Not content with sticking a toe in, Armando had plunged into his voyage, his adventure, his dream. And so had we.

Chapter 1
A Short 5 Years

(This fish means it's Fritz talking)

How often have you returned from a vacation resolved to change your locale, your lifestyle, or at least, your priorities? Mari and I were no different. After two outrageous weeks in the far southeast Bahamas, we were drunk on sunshine, saltwater and possibility. On a moonlit beach stroll, I even popped the question: "Could you see yourself living here?"

I had the name and phone number of a Nassau real estate agent handling Crooked Island properties. But before long, the comfort and discomfort of the familiar worked like a sleeping potion to dim the dream under a blanket of routine. It would be months before I came across the scrap of paper in the deep, sawdust-filled recesses of my wallet and made the call.

It had all started innocently enough with a visit to old friends now living in the Bahamas. It was February 1997, winter in Albuquerque. Mari and I had been together a year, both of us in our high forties, both divorced. We had yet to travel anywhere of consequence together. Granted, there are worse places to spend a winter than in New Mexico, but given the choice between schussing or diving, I'll take fins and snorkel any time. And if non-stop phone calls from demanding advertising clients followed by sleepless nights were any indication, Mari was a serious candidate for some R&R. What could be better, I asked her, than spending a few weeks where it was warm, affordable and remote?

There was only one requirement: bring a cooler loaded with fresh produce and protein. The only expense beyond that, Doug and Christel assured us, would be airfare since there was no place to spend money on Crooked Island. We believed them.

Tickets were booked; house, animal and business arrangements were made. We were on our way, almost. A canceled flight collapsed our itinerary and we found ourselves on our way to Nassau, New Providence, not Georgetown, Exuma, where Doug was to meet us with his Cessna 172. I used the in-flight phone to call the only number for Crooked Island we had—Gibson's Lunchroom—and woke everyone on the plane shouting a message to stop Doug before he took off.

We spent an unplanned night in Nassau, then appeared early the next morning for the twice weekly BahamasAir flight to Crooked Island. Which was canceled and rescheduled for two hours hence. Which necessitated more phone calls, more shouting. The fact that we had a cooler full of travel-weary fruit, vegetables and meat seemed to be of no concern to the airline employees. Everyone had coolers. Everyone was getting edgy.

Two hours later an emissary from a group of restless bone-fishermen also Crooked-bound approached the desk attendant and asked when the plane would leave. This seemed reasonable, as there was nothing with wings visible in the boarding area or on the tarmac. The tall, uniformed employee checked his watch. "It will leave at eleven sir, but not exactly eleven."

He was right. At 11:20 the plane taxied into view. By 11:45 we were on our way.

Neither Mari nor I had ever seen the Bahamas from the air. We were transfixed by the surreal shades of turquoise rippled with waves of white sand that covered the Bahama Banks. I had a sense of returning home—I'd sailed through these waters several times over the past twenty years and was on intimate terms with some of its shallow sandbars.

When we left the green expanse of Long Island, the sea made an abrupt change to deep indigo as we crossed the two-mile deep Crooked Island Passage. When we deplaned, a cool ten-knot breeze and clear skies eclipsed the pains of travel. Defying the odds, Doug and Christel had received our messages and were there to greet us along with their neighbor, June McMillan, who provided the transport—a blue Toyota minivan with Capistrano painted in pink on the driver's side door.

We were initially impressed with Colonel Hill's 4000-ft. airstrip, but soon after landing began to understand why it had been difficult to unearth much information about Crooked from travel guides. Our final destination lay near the end of a twenty-mile journey over an unpaved, pitted road that for two hours brutalized the suspension system of June's minivan. No buildings rose beyond a single story. No boutiques, duty-free liquor or other strip-mall dwellers, much less a strip-mall. The nearest golf course was 250 miles behind us in Nassau.

We slalomed through Colonel Hill, the island hub of government. Its scattered Caribbean-style homes were painted in flavors of pumpkin, lime, pomegranate, lemon and persimmon. Foreign odors, from swooning sweet to earthy decay, billowed through the open windows. June, a veteran of thirty winters on Crooked Island, shared anecdotes about each settlement we passed: Cabbage Hill, Fairfield, Richmond Hill. We stopped briefly at Cripple Hill to pick up Henrietta, June's ten-year-old chicken that she and her husband Don had raised since it was hatched.

Along the way, I noticed a few bare power poles sticking out of the ground at odd angles. Christel explained that personal generators and solar panels were currently the only source of electricity, but the Bahamian government promised diesel generator-powered electricity and a paved road by the following year. Then everyone laughed.

The smile on Mari's face mirrored my own and I hoped it was for the same reason. This was definitely my kind of place. Even in our rural north Albuquerque home I felt the slow squeeze of urbanization. Here there was room to breathe and, I would discover, a place still intimate with the pulse and rhythms of the ocean; a place of deep quiet, steady winds and generous people, regularly punctuated by unusual and sometimes startling events.

Until Fritz suggested a visit, it never would have occurred to me to vacation in the Bahamas. I had only a vague notion of where it? they? were. Somewhere south of Florida, in the Atlantic I was pretty sure, but that's where my knowledge ended. Although, if I'd been playing a word-association game and heard the word Bahamas, I would have fired back: drugs. Asked the same question today, a hundred words would compete for attention: lobster, barracuda, sand flies, flamingo, grouper, bougainvillea.

In 1997, I was 44 years old, divorced for the second time (a somewhat reprehensible state for a Midwestern Norwegian Lutheran gal), and the owner of a fledgling sole proprietorship, Anderson Advertising and Design. World headquarters was a

11

room attached to our kitchen. The house Fritz and I shared was down a narrow, unpaved road in Albuquerque's rural North Valley.

My staff consisted of Mary, a part-time assistant who lived in our upstairs apartment and suffered from chronic fatigue syndrome, Unis, a semi-retired bookkeeper who came every Thursday bearing freshly-made baked goods, and Leon, my German Shepherd. Mary usually woke up long enough to make a few phone calls and eat on Thursdays. Unis got the laser printer to chew up enough checks to keep it nourished. Leon was pretty much always ready for action.

My clients generally had three notable attributes: they were too quirky and high-maintenance to be tolerated by larger agencies, they liked bargain-priced work and they assumed I was at their unlimited creative beck and call. Since I happen to like quirky, high-maintenance people, was terrible at keeping track of billable hours and suffer from an exaggerated desire to please, we all got along fine. Until I decided to take a vacation.

Guilt stalked my every mile that first trip to Crooked. The sunshine, the ocean, the swaying coconut palm fronds all looked suspiciously like paradise. Our hosts were relaxed and happy in their not-quite-finished house. They fished and beachcombed more days than they tiled or plastered. I wasn't having any of it.

Confronted with time, space and no responsibilities, I kicked my Midwestern activity ethic into overdrive to make up to the world for being on vacation. I ran beaches, snorkeled reefs, got in Christel's way in the kitchen, grew suspicious of Fritz who was happy reading a book in the middle of the day.

At the time, the only telephone available was located at Marina Gibson's Lunchroom in Landrail Point. One morning, as a new form of sport-torture, I decided to call the office and see if anybody was awake, eating or barking. Christel loaned me her motorized scooter for the three-mile trip to the settlement, no doubt delighted to get me out of her house. I promised to be back in time to help with lunch and sputtered off down the road.

Gibson's Lunchroom is a Crooked Island landmark. For all the right reasons, it's the establishment most frequently written about in yachting and pilot's guides to the Bahamas. Marina Gibson is the perfect ambassador: knowledgeable about all things Crooked, a great cook, a mother to all. We'd already been introduced the day after we arrived, satisfying an unwritten mandate—new visitors to Crooked Island were expected to report to the Lunchroom for inspection within a day of arrival, a sort of courtesy Customs and Immigration.

Marina was placing a call for someone when I pulled up outside the restaurant, a tiny coral-pink bungalow shaded by a spreading sapadilly tree. She smiled and waved me to a bench in the courtyard. When her party was connected she walked over and hugged me—not the brief hug of a stranger, but the big, squeezy hug of someone who has missed you for a long time. I told her I was there to make a call but would come back when she wasn't busy. She gave me a look probably reserved for white folks who are always in a hurry. "You just got here. Sit awhile." Then she disappeared into the restaurant.

So I sat. On the edge of my chair. And checked my watch every few minutes. After ten minutes and no indication that the phone would be free anytime soon, I prepared to slip away. I poked my head in the restaurant door to tell Marina I'd come another time and saw a plate heaped with food on the table. She walked out of the kitchen carrying a pitcher of lemonade and a glass with ice. "Just a little lunch," she announced. "Sit."

"Oh. No, I'm sorry," I said. "It looks great, but I really have to get going. I promised Christel I'd get back to help with lunch."

She looked at me. Smiled. Shook her head. "You don't have to go anywhere."

And just like that, I got it. She was right. Not only did I not have to rush back to the house, I didn't have to do much of anything that two weeks. I was on vacation. The world could, and would, function without me. Somehow that knowledge got under my skin that day, then kept going until it settled deep in my bones.

My graphic design company was reasonably successful, solvent and often gratifying. But as my accounts had grown, so had the amount of time I spent puzzling over the "business" side of the business: payables, receivables, taxes of infinite variety and perversity. It kept me from the parts of the job I enjoyed the most—designing, writing copy, making clients happy—and I was continually anxious. As a former social worker, I somehow knew that making the leap into true entrepreneurship wasn't for me. I liked the business as long as I could play at it; once it started getting serious it was too much like, well, business.

Marina's words conjured dreams of a life where success was measured not by profit and loss statements but by the richness and variety of experience. When I finally did return to the office there was no going back to a life of professional servitude. Freedom tasted like conch fritters and coleslaw that day at Gibson's Lunchroom. I was hungry for more.

The phone in the real estate agent's office in Nassau was answered by a vintage British Colonial voice. Alternating between wheezes and drags on a cigarette, Dorothy Atwood obligingly told me what property was available, or in our case, not available, on Crooked Island. Nothing in our price range. Nothing on the north shore where we'd get the full benefit of the northeast trade winds and abundant reefs. She said she'd call if something came up. I hoped the hissing sound I heard in the background wasn't an oxygen tank. I found out later, it was.

Thoughts and plans for an island home faded as our daily lives consumed conscious brain space. Mari's life was one continuous deadline. The fixer-upper where we lived and worked got fixed up. I finished another novel and sent it out for its first round of rejections. The bull market was ripe for day trading and I kept up my skills as a guitar maker, taking in repairs. You might have noticed a pattern here: everything I indulged in didn't require leaving the house.

Dorothy's call came one hectic afternoon, jolting me back to the white sands and turquoise water of Crooked Island, a mental image that had been eagerly waiting for its chance to surface.

"Lot 90 on the north shore is available for $24,000. One and a quarter acres with one-hundred and fifty feet on the beach."

"Is it negotiable?"

"Not really, but if you take it I'll reduce my commission by a thousand dollars."

I pictured the scrubby bluff running along the north shore beach, the flashing green pom-poms of the silver palms cheering me on.

"Hang on," I said, and went to Mari's office. She was, of course, on the phone. I signaled to interrupt.

"What's up?" she asked.

I told her.

It took about four seconds for her eyes to turn from sky blue to teal. Then she smiled and said, "Why not?"

When the price of the lot on Crooked Island turned out to be the same amount I had stashed away after selling my former house, how could I hesitate? And it seemed only fitting to invest money from an old life into a new one. We sent a check the next day, which initiated months of paperwork exchanges since we were foreigners purchasing land in the Bahamas.

While all this shuffling was going on, Fritz and I formulated a five-year plan. We'd finish upgrading our house. I would try to find someone to work into my business as a partner and possible buyer, though I was pessimistic about the chances of selling a sole proprietorship. Best-case scenario: after the house and business sold we'd take the profits (if there were any) and build on Crooked. Summers could be spent resurrecting the 100-year old farmhouse I'd fallen for years before on Washington Island in Wisconsin. It was currently uninhabitable, but we thought time, more than money, would go a long way toward raising it (literally) from the ashes of a terrible fire.

Sounded simple, right? Strangely enough, it got even simpler.

Several months later, my office phone rang at 7 a.m. It was either Fritz's sister Carla with her usual morning check-in or an over-eager client. For the hundredth time, I wished I'd sprung for caller I.D. But that day I was lucky.

Carla and I covered the usual bases first: horses, mutual friends, relatives. When we got to Jason (Carla's step-son) and his wife, Megan, discussion ensued regarding their need for a house and an outlet for Megan's creative talent, which we agreed was currently being wasted in a dead-end job. Next up was Tanya (step-daughter), a promising young writer trapped on Hollywood's brutal sitcom treadmill. Add Carla's husband Ross, an artist we all loved and were grieving for. Only fifty-seven, he had recently been diagnosed with Alzheimer's disease. Out of this whirlwind of family issues flew the solution. The three women would take over my business: Tanya as copywriter, Megan as graphic designer, Carla on board as marketing and promotions manager. Megan and Jason could buy our house. Tanya would get to move back home to be near her father. A five-minute phone conversation was all it took to trim our five-year plan to six months. A total inside job. Of course, it was all what-ifs at first, but I've since come to believe that when you point yourself in a certain direction that is the direction you move. And so, ready or not, we did.

Chapter 2
<u>No Turning Back</u>

Confronted with imminent retirement, Mari and I adjusted priorities to accommodate the new six-month plan. Her time was consumed by getting her business ready to fly without her, mine by feasibility studies for house designs and transportation to and from the islands.

Simply put, she worked; I played.

I made daily forays to Barnes & Noble and leafed through catalogs of house plans that were generally too regional for a sub-tropical beach cottage. Takeout coffee from the attached Starbucks helped placate Mari, whose business commitments interfered with these planning stages. We had liked Doug and Christel's house but the design was too ambitious for what we had in mind. Also, Doug had often said that if he'd known how big a project his house would turn out to be, he never would have started.

Not knowing exactly what Lot 90 looked like became more of an issue, so guess who made another trip to Crooked for survey purposes? By now it was August, so I tried to convince Mari the tropic heat would be a hardship. She said the only hardship was enduring my pathetic attempts to elicit her pity. I drove to Miami, caught an early flight to Nassau on a Wednesday and made a same-day connection to Crooked.

Armed with a machete and hundred-foot tape measure, Doug and I hacked through the bush on the salt pond side of the lot. We eventually found the survey markers—globs of cement embedded with highly corroded chunks of re-bar. The oceanside markers were long gone so we measured back from the nearest ones we could find. Give or take a few inches either way, the lot measured out correctly.

From our beach rose a nearly vertical bluff of sandstone, 17 feet high. The property sloped back 450 feet to the salt pond, or as named on the map: "The Great Brine Pond." Forty feet back from the bluff came the sharpest decline, enough to make me think about a split-level house. I knew there would be some excavation involved with this design—my eyeball estimated it minor to moderate. (My eyeball rarely lets me down, but when it does...)

The property had hundreds of poisonwood trees (think poison ivy with attitude) from seedlings to the size of mature apple trees. Despite my long pants and a long-sleeved shirt I returned home with an itchy body rash that could have keynoted a dermatology conference. Even Mari was sympathetic. We hadn't yet learned about gum elemi trees, a visual cousin and natural antidote to poisonwood.

I sketched an elevation of the lot for Mari. We eventually agreed that a split-level design was the way to go: main living-quarters above with garage and guest room below.

I worked with the following design parameters:

1- 1,200 to 1,500 square feet in size
2- Variety of construction materials
3- Nothing to weigh over sixty pounds
4- Climate appropriate
5- Guest room bath
6- Materials not to exceed $25,000

I eventually came up with a design that seemed esthetically practical: post and beam construction of poured concrete for the lower walls and front upper wall. Native rock and coral would be hand-laid between uprights, with framed walls on the upper-level sides and back, cedar plywood siding and sheet-rock interior. Floor: tongue and groove pine. Ceiling: tongue and groove with a layer of insulation topped with a hipped metal roof and low-profile cupola. Most of the windows would be louvered aluminum slats with screens, plus a few fixed-glass windows and six-foot sliding glass door facing the ocean.

Compiling a materials list began in earnest, along with hours spent cruising the isles of a nearby Home Depot for ideas and prices. After crunching the numbers on the roof design I figured it would be a squeeze to come in on budget but we were both attached to the West Indian hipped-roof look so I didn't scrap it, yet.

You know how some ideas sound great at the time, but when implemented don't quite work out? Case in point: the composting toilet. Two rare commodities on Crooked are fresh water and topsoil. The ultimate solution seemed to be a composting toilet, which requires no water and generates plenty of compost. I also figured it would be less expensive than a conventional toilet and septic system. Cruising the Internet I came across a unit that would fit our needs and was even on sale. Eight hundred dollars later we had a huge box sitting on our front porch in New Mexico.

To satisfy the building committee on Crooked Island we had to submit a full set of blueprints (not white, blue), approved and stamped by a Bahamian architect. Because split-level was considered two stories, we also needed a nod from the "Multi-Story Committee" in Nassau. During the survey trip, a local contractor had given me the name of a Nassau architect. After I sent him the plans and $150, he stamped and forwarded them to

Crooked Island for final approval. From there they seemed to vanish.

Well aware of the "island time" phenomenon, I waited almost two months before calling the administrator's office. The woman who answered the phone listened politely and then asked me to hold. I hate getting put on hold at any time, but on an overseas call I can hear dollars ticking by. I was on the verge of hanging up when she came back on the line. "Are they in a long mailing tube addressed to the building committee?"

I put my hand over the receiver and briefly closed my eyes. Yes, I told her, that sure sounded like our plans. She assured me they would reach the proper officials, but didn't say when. Two weeks later I called Doug's neighbor, a member of the building committee, and was told the plans had been approved.

By now our deadline for leaving Albuquerque was only a few months away. It was time to start shopping.

Question: What's the difference between a great vacation and total life upheaval?

Answer: In my case, about a year.

While Fritz spent hours with a T-square and graph paper, large boxes began to appear on the porch. Carla and I convened a family meeting in her mountainside backyard to map out the friendly takeover of Anderson Advertising and Design. After several hours we emerged with a plan that would, we hoped, seamlessly extricate me from the business over the next several months. The new owners would pay me $5,000 a year for four years, which would buy the equipment (computers, software, office furniture, supplies), existing accounts, receivables and the intangibles like reputation, goodwill, potential, established credit. The agency name would become Anderson Ward (Carla, Tanya and Megan's surname). To keep continuity and reassure clients, I'd stay on the masthead for at least a year, even though most people knew I was, as the story went, disappearing into the Bermuda Triangle.

Three months before we planned to leave, Megan, who would be my principal replacement as graphic designer, moved with her husband Jason into our upstairs apartment. Tanya would come on board closer to departure time; the business couldn't afford her full-time salary until I was no longer taking a draw. Carla, who had a husband to care for and a museum to run, would throw what life-rings she could to the two young women as they jumped fully dressed into the deep end of the advertising business.

Could a different family have managed all this? Impossible to say, of course, but what became clear as our own story unfolded was that our richest resources were the ones closest to our hearts. Family and friends became vicarious participants in every phase of our "project" giving the whole enterprise a barn-raising atmosphere. To counterbalance, leveraging our home and my livelihood for freedom and change formed a creative vacuum that other family members could fill, enrich and expand.

And they did.

With basic design-software training, Megan's raw talent ignited—her work snapped and sparkled. Tanya arrived fresh from Los Angeles and the copywriting blasted into orbit. I began to understand the meaning of planned obsolescence.

What for Fritz was a natural extension of a life already free from convention, was for me a leap into an abyss of heady freedom. I couldn't imagine how it would feel to wake up in the morning and not have to be somewhere, doing something, for someone. While my present situation was satisfying (and often much more than that), I craved a life with unscripted possibility. I wanted to empty my mental junk drawer, then cram it full of new thoughts, experiences and surprises.

And I was more than ready to stop running into all of Fritz's old girlfriends. Never in my life had I been around someone so adored by so many ex-whatevers. Former wives (two), girlfriends from high school and college, and women who sailed with him during his ten-year circumnavigation drifted into our lives with astonishing regularity. They showed up at book club meetings, parties (at our house), and bookstores, even in the bleachers at a horse show. For a while I tried to slot them into proper chronological order, but that took too much energy.

I complained to Carla who only laughed and said, "Well, he's not a playboy, he's just had a lot of relationships." No help there.

I can see now that what bothered me the most was the Big Question: Why did none of these matches catch hold and last? (I'd been divorced, too—my two marriages had consumed twenty-three years.) I knew logistics was a big factor. His first marriage dissolved in the wake of a sailboat. The second flourished at sea but struggled on land. But try as I might, I couldn't pin anything on Fritz's past but the ability to openly embrace (literally) new people and situations, cheerfully moving on when a partnership went south. And after all, when couples connect in their forties, there has been enough time for a matched set of baggage to accumulate. I hated feeling petty and jealous and I was getting good at it.

One evening after a brutally long day of meetings, deadlines and computer crashes, I picked up a stray book, poured a glass of white wine and found a spot on the porch between the grill and composting toilet. Inside the front cover of the book, in a feminine hand, was a glowing inscription to Fritz. Thanks for the most incredible experiences of my life, etc. etc. I'll never be the same, etc., etc. Love forever, etc. etc.

I confronted him by the dining room table, shouting eloquent things like, "What difference does it make who you're with? I'm just the next one in line! If I left you'd just go out and find someone else!

He quietly replied, "If you ever decide you don't want to be with me, I won't make it hard for you to go, but I don't want to find anyone else."

I wonder now if some of my eager willingness to pull up physical, emotional and social stakes was an attempt to extend my shelf life beyond those who came before me. But while it's true that people in new relationships sometimes do things they might later regret to impress a partner, there was no mistaking the sense of authenticity, of rightness I intuitively felt about our direction. For whatever complicated collection of reasons, Fritz and I were on a shared trajectory that was daily gaining momentum, sweeping us forward toward a new life without regret, and without (I hoped) old girlfriends.

Chapter 3
<u>Rugs, Roaches & a Bathtub</u>

Crooked Island lies four hundred miles from Miami, Florida, in the far southeast Bahamas, less than a hundred miles from Cuba or Haiti. To get there you either fly or float. For us the decision was easy since a private plane was beyond our means and flying commercially severely limited our load capacity. I had spent the 1980's sailing a 35-foot cutter around the world and felt qualified to consider the boat option. And with 700 islands to explore, an ocean of fish to catch, and hey, maybe even sunken treasure ships to discover? We would float.

The only flaw in this plan was the money to buy an adequate vessel. I imagined a 35 to 45-foot powerboat, nothing yacht-y, primarily a workboat with a spacious hold. I'd heard of well-used fishing boats going for as little as $10,000 but was skeptical about the seaworthiness of such bargains. Anyway, I figured we'd need at least that much money just to start looking.

I'm a fan of visualization. I think it works because it forces me to get specific about what I really want. Once I have a clear picture I describe it on paper—an artist could draw or paint it with the same result—and tuck it away somewhere. This turns all that mental energy into something physical and gets it out into the world where it can start moving mountains. Over the years I've so often gotten what I pictured, I've had to get selective about what hangs around in my brain and winds up on paper.

Case in point: I used to be in the imported rug business, making biannual excursions to Turkey. I still had about fifteen nice pieces left from what was once a large inventory. The local rug market was awash in foreign wool. No one was buying outright so I planned to sell the pieces on consignment. Before I could, I got a call from a friend who was also a rug client. A couple from New Orleans was staying in her bed and breakfast inn and liked the rugs on the floor. Did I have any more?

"Not many, but send 'em over," I told her. "They might see something they like." It's tough to sell rugs with a small inventory. People like choices. The couple arrived and I spread each kilim, one on top of the other, so they could see each piece individually. When I finished I told them I'd go back through the pile. If they saw something they liked, I'd put it aside so they could see how it would stand on its own.

The woman waved a dismissive hand and said not to bother. I can't say I wasn't a bit disappointed. I had hoped to sell at least one. Then she whispered something to her husband. He nodded and said, "We'll take those."

I was pretty sure I'd heard it right and made some casual affirmative sounds, but all I really wanted to sputter was, "WHAT?"

I'd never sold so many rugs for so much in so short a time. The couple was building a 7,000-ft. home in Telluride, Colorado, and would have bought more rugs if I'd had them. While I hoped I presented myself as calm and professional, my inner self was bouncing off the walls as the string of zeros appeared on the check. I could already see the bow of the boat busting through the Gulf Stream chop.

I couldn't wait to ambush Mari with the news.

We fit an old camper to our GMC pickup and I headed for the Gulf Coast in search of a distress sale. Maybe an oil field workboat from Houston or a shrimper from Morgan City, Louisiana. Who knew? I'd have a look.

I spent a week poking in and out of shipyards, marinas and bayous, ending up at a friend's place in Josephine, Alabama. Rick Day (think skinny Santa) operates a small boatyard at his home and is well connected in that area. He had some ideas. We drove into Pensacola where he had friends in the salvage business. I'd been there a few years before and remembered some old Navy boats in the yard. They were still there.

One was a 38-foot ex-research vessel in sad repair, with a completely enclosed cabin. All the amenities were run entirely by an onboard diesel generator. The other was a 33-foot utility boat with a 130HP, 453 Detroit Diesel engine. It was a bit smaller than I'd planned, but all cargo space—basically a big gray bathtub with a motor. The foam-filled Kevlar hull was in fine shape and the fact that it was bulletproof and couldn't sink was a plus, too. It only drew three feet of water, a must on the shallow Bahamian Banks. The engine had been removed and refurbished by the local Detroit Diesel mechanic.

The price tag? $11,000—exactly a thousand dollars less than the check for the rugs. My visualization had done me one better; there was enough left to buy material to build the cabin. We became the proud owners of the *San Diego*. Built in 1967, she'd been a utility boat for the *USS San Diego*, a large naval supply ship. We later obtained a photo and a brief history from the Navy and kept the name because of stout bronze letters fastened to the transom. (We did try a few alternatives using the existing letters:

DAGO, NODIE, DASIE, OGDEN, GONAD, etc. Right. That's why we kept the name.)

Rick offered to haul her to his yard where I could build a cabin on the stern and fit her out for her next incarnation. Over the next six months I turned the 1200-mile trip from Albuquerque to Josephine into a commute. Mari and her twenty-five year old son, Seth, came down for the first stage of the project. Seth had just returned from a two-year stint in China where he'd been studying the language and teaching English. We were glad to have his help.

Rick had a vintage aluminum Airstream trailer parked in the nearby woods, fondly referred to as The Royal Mansion. This would be our home away from home, but not until we displaced the cockroaches that thought they had squatter's rights. It was the mother lode of entomology, but a half-dozen roach bombs later the Royal Mansion was ours.

Mari wrinkled her nose when she came in. "What's that smell?"

I thought of the toxic bombs I'd set off and said, "You don't want to know."

First order of business was to coerce *San Diego's* engine into compliance. A spaghetti-like mess of wires and controls eventually made sense. Seth ran a battery cable to the starter and the fuel tanks got a cursory cleaning with fresh fuel. The first time we hit the starter, a loud THUNK indicated seizure. A 4-foot breaker bar and big hammer finally broke the beast loose, but it refused to start. We played our ace and called Jimmy, a retired truck driver with diesel fuel for blood. Built like a fireplug with a crop of shaggy white hair, he was remarkably clairvoyant around engines and had an endless litany of tales from the road.

Jimmy listened to the engine crank then stared for a full minute. I'm sure those four pistons quivered in fear. Minutes later, he had the whole top end of the engine dismantled and the culprit dangling in his hand. One of the injectors was, not surprisingly, frozen. Several hours of intimidation, from hammer blows and heat to verbal abuse, brought the injector around to Jimmy's way of thinking. Early the next morning I reassembled the motor and without expectation, turned the key. When it roared to life I jumped back so fast I almost fell off the boat, twelve feet off the ground.

Each month I'd make a run to Alabama to continue work on *San Diego*. The sailboat I'd taken around the world was now an exhibit at Tinkertown Museum just outside Albuquerque. Before each trip south I pilfered nautical necessities from the old girl: bronze water tanks, electrical switches, solar panel, chain, anchors, winches, compass, line, navigation equipment and countless fittings and fastenings. Without this little gold mine, the fitting-out of *San Diego* would have seriously strained our budget.

I got to work on an 8-ft. x 8-ft. stern cabin. Inside, I squeezed a galley with sink and two-burner gas stove, a full-sized bed that shifted into a settee during the day, a navigation station and a five cubic-foot freezer. The hardest part was selling Mari on the Porta-Potty that slid under the bunk.

Mari and Seth returned for the final stage and *San Diego's* launching party. We laid on her debut colors: school bus yellow for the hull, dark blue trim and white superstructure. After ten years in mothballs she was back in the water, but with little sign of her naval heritage. She looked like what she was meant to be, a mini-freighter.

Skip this section if you've always agreed with your partner's decisions, if your tastes in habitat and furnishings dovetail in perfect harmony, if major change in your life has always developed to match the carefully composed picture in your head.

Fritz called from Florida with two boat options. One sounded good. She was a former navy research vessel complete with head and shower, galley, a couple of cabins—pretty much my priorities in descending order. I gave this boat an immediate romantic spin, already projecting life aboard a soon-to-be handsome expedition yacht. I imagined her seaworthiness, her attractive lines, the pretty picture we'd make motoring into a far distant port. The idea of that boat fit neatly into my concept of a proper transition from business owner/career woman into, what, cruising babe? She sounded like a floating home I could live on and like.

The second option was *San Diego*: a few feet shorter, a slightly smaller engine, and a few thousand dollars less. On the phone, Fritz explained what those differences could mean when it came to budget, maintenance and maneuverability, lobbying for *San Diego* with an experienced captain's foresight. I hadn't a sea-leg to stand on to defend my fantasy. Score one for practical.

You could fill a marina with what's already been written about the trouble couples get into around boats. Relationships that have negotiated equal footing on land often pitch into dangerous troughs when tested at sea. Or long before they reach the sea. And while there are plenty of women who have expertise around boats, whether operating, maintaining, or repairing, I was not one of them. The decision to buy *San Diego* was the first of many times I would defer to Fritz's experience. Though this clearly made sense, it began to brew a new level of complexity into our relationship.

In fact, complex is a dandy word to describe my thoughts when I found myself in the Pensacola salvage yard amidst piles of helicopter parts, boat detritus and mud. A slight breeze floated the smell of diesel fuel more efficiently than any of the surrounding engine carcasses could manage.

Perched overhead on a stand—boats out of the water are "on the hard"—under a canopy of shedding live oak trees, was what looked like a reject from a plus-sized bumper boat carnival ride.

"Cool, Fritz!" my son said.

Fritz grinned with a captain's pride and began to rig *San Diego* for the forty-mile road trip to the rehab yard. Like any first mate worth her salt, I climbed aboard and started to rake.

Later, at the Royal Mansion, after the cockroach corpses were swept aside, I popped the cork on the bottle of champagne we'd bought and carried it out to the yard. Already Seth and Fritz were high up on the boat conferring over some puzzling detail involving circuits, hook-ups or missing parts.

Fritz had chosen long ago not to have children. His standard explanation: "I'm too selfish to give up time for kids." I wasn't so sure about that as I witnessed the give and take of the two men finding their way into friendship. As two vastly different personalities, there was and will always be occasional collisions of opinion, emotion and hormones.

Seth, at 25, had weathered two divorces with me. That he could still so generously adapt to this radical change in my life left me breathless. In fact, months before when I had gotten snagged on a dangling piece of apprehension it was my son who said, "Go for it, Mom. When will you ever get another opportunity like this?"

Witnessing the evolution and growth of my family in its many forms was both gift and lesson that summer. The lesson? If the important relationships in my life were getting the nourishment they needed (including my relationship with myself), all the other details would somehow find their way into balance. Which worked well for everything except that damn Porta-Potty.

Chapter 4
<u>Goodbye and Hello</u>

Mari and I were married on September 30, 1998, at the home of friends in Corrales, New Mexico. It was a simple outdoor ceremony under a fall-blazed cottonwood, presided over by Stan Alexander, a local psychic who also held a doctorate in theology. We liked the balance. Stan made no dire predictions about our relationship or personal welfare. I guess that meant we were ready for life aboard a small boat.

We spent the next two weeks ripping up roots, some painful, some not. I'd had lots of experience moving around and mine came up as easily as radishes in sand. Not so Mari. She was more like a giant cottonwood in clay. First there was Seth, who was usually traveling to some remote part of the globe learning obscure languages. For once in his adult life he was spending time in Albuquerque living in his VW van (complete with flowered mandalas) and now Mari would be the one to leave.

Next came Bubba, a cantankerous gray gelding she'd rescued from an abusive home fifteen years before. He was now twenty and, understandably, a bit stiff and grumpy. This was a horse that would be tough to give away, much less sell. Fortunately a good friend offered to take him and Bubba retired to a paddock only a mile from his existing home.

Then there was Leon, a ninety-pound German shepherd/lab cross who was all blond shepherd in looks and demeanor, and none more handsome. He'd been Mari's constant companion for all of his six years and she agonized over whether or not to take him along.

Here was a middle-aged dog that disliked water and loud noises, facing weeks at a time aboard a small boat with a raucous motor. There was no question that he would follow her lead, but at what price? The debate—companionship versus quality of life—raged in her mind. She had two offers for good homes; one was Jason and Megan, who were purchasing our house and one-third of her business. No change in living quarters was a big plus, but ultimately it was Stan Alexander's psychic blessing that persuaded Mari to leave Leon in his existing home.

I was the one who took the dregs of the family heirlooms to the flea market. I believed Mari incapable of that particular chore, especially when she almost shed tears over the red Weber grill.

Two years before Fritz and I had gotten together, I'd applied to become a volunteer in the Big Sisters program. As part of an extensive screening process, potential candidates were required to take a psychological profiling test, which would, hopefully, uncover any latent desires to harm children. When the smiling social worker handed me my results (nothing lurking in my psychic closet) I began to see why so many of my internal conversations sounded like good cop-bad cop interrogations from a B-grade detective flick.

While the test claimed I was bold, adventurous and willing to try new things, it also wagged a cautionary finger just in case I thought shedding some skin was going be painless. Battling it out for equal time was 1) tendency to worry, 2) strong sense of obligation, 3) emotionally sensitive, and 4) tender-minded.

The Weber grill was just the beginning.

Those bits and pieces of domestic life I wasn't able to sacrifice were packed in boxes for storage. A pair of stained-glass windows I'd bought at a farm auction, a succession of Seth's school photos (from short hair, to punk hair, to ponytail, back to short), two boxes of Christmas ornaments from my childhood, a tin wall sconce Seth made in Cub Scouts. We also packed rugs, some art, a few special books.

Our wedding became symbolic not only of commitment, but also of passage and change. Like going off to college, leave-taking was profoundly bittersweet. I knew my son and I would always be part of each other's lives; I also knew he was at a particularly sensitive point in his. And as sure as I was that he was capable of moving forward on his own and in fact would grow through the experience, part of me wanted to stay, be there, be his mother, keep him safe. He had the maturity to reverse roles and gently push me out of the nest.

Bubba and I had shared years of trails, jumps and battles of will. I had him to thank for one broken arm (kicked) and two concussions (bucked). I knew I'd miss the crabby old bastard but it was Leon who never let go of my heart. I could not ask him to come with me, but life without a dog felt incomplete. Fortunately, before too long, that would change.

We moved aboard *San Diego* on October 18th. She would be our home for the next 87 days. After ten days of final tweaking, the boat was fully ready. Three solar panels and two alternators kept separate banks of batteries charged with both 12 and 24-volt systems. An inverter gave us 110-volt power for the freezer and microwave oven. We raised a 25-foot mast from a tabernacle mounted near the bow. This would act as a cargo boom and carry a small riding sail to help steady the boat's motion in a seaway.

After the curtains were hung in the cabin, *San Diego* looked downright homey. The composting toilet, a boxed 10-ft x 20-ft canvas garage, a Honda motor scooter and a bicycle took a healthy bite out of the storage space, and we hadn't even started shopping for Crooked. We had yet to discover the voracious appetite of *San Diego's* hold.

We spent this time in a quiet bayou, tied to the jetty in front of a friend's house. Nick and Corrine couldn't have been kinder, and along with Rick Day, helped with nautical refinements and cold beer. We had access to fresh water, an outdoor shower and a downstairs toilet.

At noon on October 29th we left for the 650-mile shakedown cruise to Fort Lauderdale, Florida, via the Okeechobee Waterway. Nick motored his skiff alongside for a half-mile so Corrine could take photos, then they saluted, turned for home and we were on our own.

Most of this run would be in the Intercoastal Waterway, commonly called "The Ditch." Since we weren't well acquainted with the engine yet, if it had an obnoxious streak I preferred a confrontation in protected waters. It wasn't until much later, after entering the Bahamas, that we found the confidence to call the engine our friend.

For three days, scenery inched by at 8mph. Close confines and heavy barge traffic in The Ditch meant we couldn't use the autopilot. Whenever we were underway, one of us steered from the helm and monitored the heat and oil gauges. I waited for the slightest complaint from the engine, keeping my own gauges in the green with cold drinks. I was almost disappointed when she didn't miss a stroke—all that wasted energy. We anchored at night beyond the marked channel and relished the abrupt silence after the SHUT DOWN lever was pulled.

I was skittish about venturing onto the big pond—the Gulf of Mexico. The 250-mile open water passage across the Gulf from Apalachicola to Ft. Myers, Florida, would be a first for Mari and *San Diego*. I hoped they would both take well to the sea. The harbor was calm the morning we left and darned if it didn't stay that way until we reached Ft. Myers the following day—a glass-top run from shore to shore. The engine didn't miss a lick and I no longer tiptoed. Mari spent her night watches stargazing, a pastime reserved for those with good sea legs. The autopilot steered the entire way and our fishing gear began to pay for itself with a freezer-sized mackerel and meal-sized tuna. The hundred dollar GPS also proved itself trustworthy, guiding us faultlessly to the desired landfall. The only glitch appeared in the 12-volt charging system, which actually put me at ease. Passages on small boats are rarely trouble-free, and this was a problem easily handled.

The Okeechobee Waterway bisects Florida from Ft. Myers on the west, through Lake Okeechobee to Stuart on the east coast. Indiantown lies ten miles beyond Lake Okeechobee's east side. It would be our stateside base for *San Diego* in the years to come.

The lake is sixty feet above sea level necessitating a series of locks that act as hydraulic elevators to lift and lower boat traffic. This is where *San Diego* excelled. With the thick rubber bumpers that lined her rails, there was nothing we could do that would damage her hull—watch out all you spit and polish guys, we're comin' thru!

While crossing Lake Okeechobee we performed speed/economy tests and found that at 1,450 RPMs we reached eight miles per hour and used only two gallons of diesel fuel per hour. Each mile per hour after that consumed an additional gallon of fuel—our top speed of eleven mph used five gallons of fuel per hour.

Remember Jimmy, the diesel wizard? Before we left Alabama, he had sold us a trailer that would hold all six tons of *San Diego* and even offered to deliver it and our truck to Indiantown. Sure enough he was there to meet us when we tied up at the marina's fuel dock the morning of November 5th. Topping off our good luck, when I asked at the marina office for someone to repair the 12-volt alternator, the man to see was standing in front of me.

Not an hour later, I plugged into shore power without turning off the on-board inverter (I didn't want to interrupt the freezer cycle) and the polarity reversed, frying the inverter.

Expensive Lesson Number 1: *Think Twice, Act Once.*

Three days at the marina saw everything shipshape, including Mari, who had grown weary of the solar shower and reveled in the high water pressure ashore. And the Porta-Potty? Well, it just seemed to grow on us and for the small amount of time it was in use, the cabin became the most spacious head I've ever seen on such a small boat.

Hold it (pun intended) right there. The Porta-Potty did not grow on me. We did not bond. We never became close. And it was only in use for small amounts of time because, a) I never knew how long I had between a pitch (ass over teakettle) or a roll (teakettle over ass), and b) as a representative of a gender physically disposed to sit-preferred processes of elimination, I learned to move fast—the cabin was a shared space after all—efficiently, or not at all.

The underlying issue, of course, was privacy. Bathrooms are a feminine institution. Locked door + hot bath + cup of tea = peace, calm, recharge. Mirrors might be a poor substitute for true self-reflection, but it's nice to know if the face staring back looks familiar. While the marina's bathroom had two out of the above three attributes, baths were fast joining mountains and deserts as fond memories. The tiny, cement-floored cubicle also invariably had a line of women equally eager, I suspect, for a few moments alone.

Of the entire boat experience, marina life was the hardest for me to adapt to. It felt like grown-up camp with self-appointed counselors who enforced tricky and elusive rules. I was forever using the wrong bucket at the wrong spigot or trying to fill a water tank with a soaker hose. Was I overly sensitive? Undoubtedly. But since leaving New Mexico my identity labels had been peeling off one by one, sinking in bayous, blowing out to sea or winding up as egret's nest fluff along the waterway. Caught without the confidence the familiar inspires I felt exposed, vulnerable and just bloody stupid in many situations, but not all. It turned out I took pretty well to the water.

It's 2 a.m., my watch for the next two hours. Fritz is asleep in the cabin behind me. We're in the Gulf of Mexico, somewhere between what we left and where we're going. I'm in the captain's chair, feet propped on the engine cover, alternately scanning gauges and the surrounding dark for red or green lights that would indicate another vessel. The sky is clogged with stars, some pulsing in place, others arcing toward earth. San Diego has slipped me in between water and sky, into what might as well be outer space. It's like a backstage pass to a celestial magic show, with the engine's reassuring rumble grounding an otherwise surreal sensation of suspended animation.

We would make eight trips on *San Diego* to and from Crooked Island over the next four years. There were countless consciousness-expanding nights following that first one. But ultimately, it wasn't an ability to embrace new experiences or withstand discomfort that forecast my success around boats. It was guts. Not bravery. Stomach. Not getting seasick meant I could fully participate in situations where both crew were needed; winching the dinghy onto the cabin roof in a churning 2-ft. chop was a challenge but not intestinal hell. We were not always skilled labor, my stomach and I, but we could be counted on to show up for work. (That's Fritz you hear cheering.) I learned to tie knots, fill a bucket with seawater while underway (harder than it sounds), reel in dinner, steer the boat through quartering seas. In time, footing I had however temporarily lost on land I regained at sea, a blessed balance.

If my identity labels were disappearing in *San Diego's* wake, it seemed there were new ones attaching themselves that were stickier, even waterproof.

Chapter 5
"You want this shipped where?"

"The Ditch" on a weekend is a true horror. For two days *San Diego* bucked and cavorted in monster wakes churned up by flashy cigarette boats and macho sport fishermen. (Give me a gale at sea any day.) By the time we reached West Palm Beach, we'd had enough and opted for the outside route for the forty-five mile run to Ft. Lauderdale. With a 15-knot onshore breeze and four-foot seas, *San Diego* rocked and rolled for six delightful hours as the autopilot steered and we reeled in a half-dozen tuna. The steadying sail worked like a charm in the beam sea and we looked forward to the 400-mile trip to Crooked Island.

Over the previous few months I'd been in regular contact with Cooter (real name), a shipping agent we had lined up to transport the bulk of our building materials to Crooked Island. He'd given me directions to the Port of Dania where his offices were located and said he'd meet us there. We found the right canal just south of Ft. Lauderdale and motored a mile inland to a thriving commercial port packed with small freighters and barges bound for the Bahamas. Though late in the day, the basin sweltered under a shroud of diesel fumes and low-tide stench.

We reversed course and retreated to a sail-up bar we'd passed on the way in. I ordered two beers, found a phone, and left a message for Cooter that we'd meet him at ten the following morning. At the mouth of the canal we tied up to an abandoned barge for the night and hoped we wouldn't get rousted by the water police.

Cooter, a portly good ol' boy in his sixties, turned up about 10:30 a.m. By then we'd been nearly asphyxiated by the basin's bad air but his charm dispelled most of the fog. Until he called me Fritzy. I understood it was down-home bonhomie, but it still rankled. Cooter recommended the Hollywood, FL, municipal marina as a good place to park the boat and said we could borrow his truck the next day to retrieve ours in Indiantown, a generous offer that almost made Fritzy sound okay.

Two miles and as many low bridges to the south, we nosed into Slip 24, which would be our home for the next two weeks. Renee, the harbormaster, was a fit blond in her thirties who Mari instantly liked. After fifteen days on *San Diego* she craved exercise and Renee needed a workout partner. I was off the hook.

Waiting for Cooter became a major pastime and phone calls rarely helped, but this was nothing compared to pinning him down on the details of the shipping venture. He had originally told me he could run a load out to Crooked for about $10,000. I assumed that if we found others to share the barge, the price per person would go down. Now we found out that wasn't the case—it would all be based on weight and volume. Mari and I were both alarmed at this reinterpretation. We had $6,000 to spend for shipping. If it was going to cost a bit more, we would have to make other arrangements. Cooter told us not to worry about it.

Expensive Lesson Number 2: *Get Everything In Writing*.

Now we worried about our future neighbor, Bruce, who had agreed to share the barge and split the $10,000 fee. He was en route to Florida and we had no way to alert him to this pricing change. There were also other folks on Crooked having miscellaneous cargo brought out; fortunately we were able to reach them with the news.

Our container was another issue. We'd bought a used one, from Cooter, that wasn't immediately available, meaning we couldn't pack it as we shopped. "No problem, Fritzy." Draw up a loading diagram and give it to the warehouse manager, he told us, and it'll be followed to the letter.

Expensive Lesson Number 3: *Pack Your Own Container.*

Next morning, we spent the entire trip to Indiantown trying to decide if we should find another shipper. It didn't help that the "door open" buzzer on Cooter's truck wouldn't shut off. Bzzzzzzzzzzzzz!

An essential component of our agreement was on-site delivery of our building materials. Cooter promised an all-terrain forklift and flatbed trailer for the three-mile transfer from barge to building site. This was a major consideration since we'd be shipping more than twenty pallets of concrete products, not to mention huge bundles of lumber, plywood and sheet rock.

We finally reached Bruce, who thought Cooter might be still better than other, possibly worse, alternatives. We agreed, and started shopping.

Once on Crooked, the supply line was closed. Every detail of construction had to be precisely planned; every board, fixture, screw and socket pre-purchased. Doug's story about having to fly to a neighboring island for a handful of roofing nails was a good reminder.

We allotted a full day of shopping for each major materials category. The first day we spent eight hours in electric, the next, plumbing, and so on, filling cart after cart. Since it was an export order, the folks at Home Depot assigned us a knowledgeable person in each department. Almost immediately, my original list was steamrolled by all kinds of new and great stuff, and we shot over budget. Our hip-roof design fell victim to cuts and was changed on the fly to gabled ends with no cupola. The savings? Over $1000. Mari was especially disappointed, but on the upside, we gained more ceiling height, which translated into visual spaciousness.

After ten days of this we could have been punching the employee clock—few staff members knew the store better than we did.

Next up was a morning at Security Aluminum for louvered windows followed by a long afternoon at BrandsMart to select appliances. Ironically, the most difficult thing to find was a gas stove that didn't require electricity. Even though Crooked had recently gotten electricity, the power source was a huge diesel generator three miles from our building site. No one could predict how reliable it would be. After each purchase, we made arrangements to have the items sent to Cooter's office. He also got copies of all our receipts so deliveries could be confirmed before the barge left port.

Much of the Bahamas had recently suffered extensive hurricane damage prompting their government to suspend the duty on all imported building materials. This would save us a bundle, but we needed a letter from Crooked's administrator to qualify us for the exemption. Numerous faxes to his office went unacknowledged. The afternoon before our departure, Mari tried one last time to reach him by phone. Amazingly, she did, only to hear him say we'd have to see him in person before he'd issue the letter. We'd have to take our chances with customs without it.

A final trip to Sam's Club for food was enough to breach our emotional limit. The sanity saver was Dos Equis beer for $2.38 a *case*.

Before leaving Albuquerque, friends had asked how I'd tolerate being "first mate" on much of this journey. (I'd already dipped my toe in those waters when Fritz found the boat.) I was used to commanding my own little ship. Now instead of giving directives, I'd often be taking them, dependent on Fritz not just for knowledge and experience, but when at sea, for my life.

But if it wasn't equal, at least it felt fair. And it was surprisingly comforting to support, assist and apprentice, trading responsibility for "other duties as assigned."

Which didn't mean there weren't ground rules, notably:

1. If the captain yells, the mate will not respond.

2. If the mate is slow, the captain is well-advised to be patient. Impatience will cause a work stoppage.

3. When the mate whacks her head on the cargo boom (again) the captain will refrain from comment.

4. When the captain whacks his head on the cargo boom (again) he will refrain from hollering high-volume expletives if the mate is asleep in the cabin, or, if she is not.

5. In the future, if the captain or the mate drives past a Home Depot, he/she will promise to keep going.

Until November 1998, I thought triathlons were the ultimate test of strength and endurance. Wrong. Two weeks of shopping in south Florida would have easily qualified us for a shopping Ironman. At Home Depot, our personal trainer was Angela, a sweet-voiced young woman from the import department. Angela never quite figured out where Crooked Island was ("You want this shipped where?"), but she kept the wooden pallets, shrink-wrap and coffee coming, enough to overflow barge and bladder. When I'd stumble out of the product fray at various intervals during the day, it was Angela who'd smile, spin me around, shove me back in.

In plumbing, electric and lumber I was list-handler, inventory tracker and mule. In lighting, paint and accessories I lobbied, negotiated and whined. Where once I would have spent hours choosing one lamp or bedspread or wall color, I now pointed, yanked, stacked and wrapped. Whatever vision I'd once had for the house became blurred by so many decisions in so short a time.

Fritz, whose normal walking pace is more amble than stride, found another gear in Home Depot, no doubt fueled by nervous energy. He disappeared around corners and vanished down aisles, coming finally to roost facing walls covered with circuit breakers or outlets or PVC connectors. There he would sink deep into contemplation, completely immobile. I once drove a half-mile to a Subway for tuna sandwiches and made it back before he moved.

These methods particular to our madness—building the house ourselves, using a boat for transportation—were chosen because of Fritz's background. Most of what was required either tapped skills he already possessed or could add through research, struggle or some of both. It gave us a head start and the chance to build the momentum we'd need to portage around the rough spots.

Through the years we'd meet other couples (or solos) who'd opted out of more traditional lives. No one did it the same way. Those with more money hired others to smooth their transition. Those with less often took more time. Some flew instead of floating. One couple rented their stateside home while they built in the islands—monthly income with the freedom to be elsewhere.

What we all shared was a willingness to allow curiosity and conscious choice to evolve our lives into explorations of new territory without prescribed boundaries. The most successful relationships had found fluid balance. Depending on the situation either partner could step forward, back or to the side with agility, and without ego.

At the end of two weeks Fritz and I had amassed a do-it-yourself home kit, missing only a set of instructions. We had a heavily loaded boat, an uncertain weather forecast and four hundred miles to go before the real work began.

Chapter 6
<u>Slogging East</u>

It's November 23rd, departure day. San Diego squats four inches below her waterline. Aboard are six months worth of provisions, building supplies for our pre-barge infrastructure and 400 gallons of fuel and water. So much for her earlier innocence and gay buoyancy. Now she's a workin' girl.

We saluted our new friends at the Hollywood City Marina and cruised south through Miami's glitz to Key Biscayne's No Name Harbor. It was the first night in two weeks without the wild hoopla from the Greek restaurant across from the marina.

NOAA weather predicted we'd meet 10 to 15-knot winds and two to four-foot seas across the Gulf Stream the next day. We hoisted the dinghy onto the roof of the cabin—Mari on winch and me on muscle—to prepare for the crossing. From my decade at sea I had already learned that it's not a matter of *if* a dinghy towed on an open-water passage will get swamped or snap the painter (tow line), it's *when*.

At first light, pre-departure jitters—a carry-over from sailing days—began to writhe in my guts like a coiled python. I slammed down some coffee and hauled up the anchor before Mari was even awake. I knew the roar of the engine had ruined her plans for a quiet breakfast, but the snake was squeezing and wouldn't let go until we were well under way. While most of these jitters came from my respect for the sea and Mother Nature, they were also a reaction to the responsibility required of the captain.

We nosed out of the harbor and met the Atlantic swells. *San Diego* felt a bit sluggish on the rise—not surprising considering her load. I noticed a few clouds around, felt a slight breeze from the east and relaxed at the helm with a second cup of coffee. The chart said it was forty-five miles to Cat Cay and our GPS (Global Positioning System) agreed. I punched in a few coordinates and instantly knew our heading, speed and ETA. What a change from the days when celestial navigation, a radio direction finder and pair of binoculars were the only feasible means of finding your way around the globe in a small boat.

The first squall hit at 11 a.m. with eye-stinging rain. A fresh wind from the east threw up steep five-foot seas and *San Diego* plowed straight through them, shipping walls of white foam over the bow. A dip in the ammeter showed the bilge pump was hard at work. We backed off to four knots to keep San Diego's nose out of the waves and retreated to the cabin's relative quiet while the Gulf Stream kicked up its heels. Every so often we'd launch off a rogue swell and slam into the trough of the next wave, like a diving U-Boat. Each time it looked like we'd meet Davy Jones, San Diego's flared bow would lurch for the sky in a cascade of green seas. The steady 20-knot wind kept our forward speed to a crawl. We counted the minutes to Cat Cay.

The island finally hove into view at four p.m. Now the pressure was on to clear customs before overtime charges kicked in at five o'clock. We were also concerned about not having the duty-exempt letter from Crooked's administrator—a potential jackpot for customs.

I breezed into the office with fifteen minutes to spare but it was clear the officer had no intention of leaving his air-conditioned cocoon to inspect our boat. A painless, and I hoped auspicious, encounter.

In the morning we continued east over the Bahama Banks, a ninety-mile stretch of clear shallow water churned-up by 15 to 20-knot winds. We again slowed *San Diego* to four knots and the hours pounded by. By 8 p.m. we'd had enough. I tossed out the anchor and the boat bucked through the night in the middle of the banks. By morning the wind eased and the seas flattened and we sprinted the sixty miles to Nassau for Thanksgiving dinner.

Rough days at sea are like childbirth. Uncomfortable as hell while you're laboring through them, all but forgotten when you're delivered safe into port. Still, I'll never again buy a ticket to ride a roller coaster. *San Diego* may not have been my idea of a smooth and handsome trawler, but as wet and tossed about as I often was, I never felt unsafe. Pick any other emotion (no need to leave out homicidal) and I'll raise my hand. For the most part I was too busy catching torpedoing potatoes, stuffing clothes between bottles of olive oil and wine or coating eggs with Vaseline to worry too much about unscheduled swims.

144 eggs. No refrigeration. No problem, sayeth my beloved. Simply coat each one with a layer of petroleum jelly to seal the pores and the eggs will last if not forever, at least for several months, long enough to be eaten. We had flats of eggs under the settee in the cabin, eggs tucked in the forward hold, eggs nestled between sacks of concrete and stacks of lumber to prevent

premature scramble. Once coated, it was a long thirty-three feet from aft to fore with a tray of newly greased eggs carried by newly greased hands. With water cascading over the bow at irregular intervals and the slippery path to the food-storage hold blocked by boxes, bags and barrels, timing was everything and never quite right.

I wasn't so sure this oil product scheme would work, but Fritz's voice of experience assured me only a few would go rotten. I really hoped those would be the ones he'd crack.

Tucked into the corner where Potter's Cay dock juts into Nassau Harbor and conch stands serve native cuisine late into the night, East Bay Marina slowly corrodes. Once gushing fuel pumps suck on empty tanks and electricity is only available from a creative splice. A pay phone eats quarters and laughs. Twin showers vie for water pressure and toilets have gone missing, but the folks are darn nice. *San Diego* fit right in with the riffraff on this rickety set of finger piers that required an absurd level of self-esteem to call itself marina.

During our first trip to Crooked, we'd seen a small, flat-nosed pickup truck. It looked like a big Tonka toy that converted to a flatbed—you've seen them in Asian films. It was Korean-made and sold in Nassau by Bahamas Bus and Truck. Before leaving Albuquerque I'd called the dealer and bought one over the phone, on sale. It would be perfect, we thought, not only for transportation, but also for hauling all manner of cargo. Also, since it was purchased in the country, it was duty-free.

When the salesman drove it to the marina for us to inspect, we made arrangements to have it sent to Crooked on the mail-boat. We spent a day and a half negotiating Nassau on foot to chase down insurance, pay property taxes and add even more supplies.

It was a relief to escape the cruise-ship cacophony of Nassau harbor for the forty-mile leg to the Exumas. By the time we reached Norman's Cay, a full moon lit the white crescent beach as if it were awash in reflective paint.

Since good light is a must for most navigation in the Bahamas, winter's short days made for equally short runs. As we picked our way southeast along the Exuma chain, a high-pressure ridge began to build, translating into increased easterly winds. After three days the ridge became stationary, pumping in winds of 20 to 25 knots. Boisterous seas from deep water surrounding Exuma Sound rumbled against the barrier islands. Geysers erupted when waves struck the rocky shoulders of the boat passages leading to the banks, creating a tumbled confusion of water—a tantrum in a bathtub. On the occasions we were forced to transit them, *San Diego* gyrated like a hyperactive disco queen.

In the midst of one reef-strewn cauldron the engine missed its first stroke, then faltered and dropped to a precarious idle. With virtually no headway, the ferocious rip current sent us toward the rocks. I frantically pumped the power lever hoping to free an imagined obstruction, finally coaxing from the beast a single mild roar. Enough of those and we'd have the equivalent of a steady growl, better than the current purr.

So it went, coaxing and cajoling until we cleared the pass and limped to the nearest anchorage. Here was the long-awaited quirk in the engine. Up until now, the motor had been too perfect. Like a person who never misses, it was cause for suspicion. Once at anchor, we troubleshot the system and discovered that *San Diego's* wild contortions had stirred up sludge from a near-empty fuel tank, clogging the filters. Once these were changed the motor was back to its old perfect self and I reeked of diesel fuel.

Finally. Its hidden flaw was revealed and I could relax.

I do not like the sound of the engine sputtering and then dying when I'm on board a boat imitating a washing machine on the "extra heavy-duty" cycle. Hurtling toward rock walls is unsettling —what about all those eggs?—but even worse is the sound of the captain saying, "Oh, *no*."

Fritz says "Oh, no," with the same inflection and level of alarm whether he's losing a key or losing a finger. For him, disaster is not relative to degree. There were three phases to each problem we encountered on (or off) the boat. I started to feel better once I deciphered the pattern.

Discovery: "Oh, no."

Acknowledgment: "Fuck!"

Solution: "Maybe if I..."

Sometimes I could offer a quick fix: "Here's your finger, honey." If the glitch was more technical, I stood by with screwdrivers, engine filters or Band-Aids until the wrong was righted, the stars came out and the mermaids once again sang in tune. And, knock on scales, they always did.

For three days we battled our way south, played the tides and furrowed the sand in the shallow lee of the Exumas while punching into near-gale easterlies. Until we reached the south end of Long Island we'd be in relatively protected waters and hoped the wind would ease by the time we reached the point. But it howled for days, raising monster seas. Frustrated and tired, we waited behind Long Island with only the tantalizing thirty-mile wide Crooked Island Passage keeping us from our goal.

We were not alone. Several Haitian fishing boats and a mail-boat also waited for the wind and seas to subside. The Passage was no place for the heavily laden *San Diego*.

The bay where we'd anchored was quite shallow and *San Diego* sat a hundred yards from shore. Each day we swam to the beach for an excursion inland. Local folks were happy to offer rides; over the six-day wait we got acquainted with half the population between Clarencetown and Gordon's at the south end.

Our botanical education began on Long Island. Far more agricultural than Crooked, Long Islanders have cultivated produce for generations: limes, bananas and giant papayas that look like smooth elongated pumpkins. Our first ride was courtesy of the mail-boat delivery lady. She drove past miles of stone walls, some intact and strong, some crumbling. Still embarrassingly naive with regard to Bahamian history, I asked how so many walls had come to be built. "Slaves," she said, and drove on.

We passed acres of cultivated orchards and fields. When we told her we planned to start a garden, she dropped us near a hilltop nursery. For an hour, Mr. Cartwright explained the process of fruit-tree grafting, a faster and more reliable way to start saplings. We bought three limes and a sapadilly, a beautiful spreading tree that produces a grainy pear-like fruit. Banana trees are started from suckers that sprout beside mature trees, he told us. For bananas we should see the Carrolls.

Three generations were at home when we stopped in the next day. While Mr. Carroll led Fritz to the banana grove, I stayed in the house to visit with his mother, wife and daughter. It was a warm day but the shutters were closed and the house was dark. Something had recently been baked in the kitchen.

While the grandmother silently plaited a basket from silver palm fronds, Mrs. Carroll placed a photo album in my lap. She began to talk while she slowly turned the pages. First was a snapshot of a round-faced baby with chestnut skin and ribboned hair. Next, a girl of ten or twelve in a skiff, hand on the tiller. On the last page a smiling young woman in a cap and gown.

This beloved daughter, a nursing student in Nassau, had died three weeks before. Not in Nassau, her mother whispered, as if still not believing it. She's been right there on Long Island, in a truck with friends. It was late. Her friends said she stood in the truck bed and fell out when it lurched forward. She hit her head on the pavement and died.

The grandmother spoke without looking up from her basket. They had worried sick about her in Nassau. It was rough and dangerous and they couldn't wait for her to get home. Her granddaughter had been an artist. Would I like to see her work?

There were papers stacked on a high closet shelf in the girl's bedroom. I was tallest so I reached past her clothes to bring down the drawings. Each one was of angels wearing brilliant colors, flying high over the water.

We returned to the beach late one afternoon after a day of traipsing and touring. Two women stood looking out at *San Diego*. Both German, one owned a restaurant in Deadman's Cay, the other woman was her companion. They were there purchasing grouper from an island fisherman. They were puzzled about the absence of a dinghy on shore. We explained about swimming—the dinghy was better left on the cabin roof, ready for an early departure when the wind died.

"But there are sharks!" the restaurant owner said with alarm. "The grouper are running and the fish are cleaned here. There are many sharks!"

This was not something Mari wanted to hear. I'd had experience swimming with sharks and the woman's declaration didn't bother me too much, but the look on Mari's face did. I offered to fetch the dinghy but she knew launching it was a two-person job. It was a long swim to the boat that day, but luckily, it was the last.

In the morning the wind didn't whine in the rigging and the clouds appeared less like runaway trains in the sky. We decided to poke our nose out and try to cross the passage, giving the south point, where the seas meet conflicting currents, a five-mile berth before swinging east. The Atlantic swells were mountainous but not steep and breaking. San Diego rose smoothly to every wet challenge, but we cut our speed and hand-steered over peaks and through valleys.

Scattered showers stung our eyes as we searched the horizon for the lighthouse on Bird Rock. After five tense hours we spotted the lighthouse, two more and we tucked into the lee of Crooked Island. It was December 5th.

Safe. Drenched. Exhausted. Home?

Chapter 7
Slash & Burn

Doug and Christel arrived to help offload our supplies at the Landrail Point jetty, a wave-eroded slab of concrete embellished on all surfaces with rusty rebar spurs and tangled wire mesh. It was like tying up to a metal porcupine. Combined with the continual surge from the Atlantic swells, *San Diego's* heavy-duty rub rails were severely tested. It was high tide, so with careful timing we could toss cargo across the gap between boat and jetty. Unloading at low tide would have added a three-foot upward hoist. Near the end of the transfer the boat came up so hard on her mooring lines one of the twelve-inch bronze cleats ripped clean out of the deck.

It took four trips with their 1972 Chevy station wagon—the largest ever built and fondly known as *"The Pimpmobile"*—to shift *San Diego's* cargo to the edge of our lot. Doug loved this car. He could fit an entire 4x8-ft. sheet of plywood in the back and still close the window. For the first week on Crooked, the only way we could tell our future home from the surrounding bush was by the tarp-covered mound at the side of the road.

Each morning we left the boat at anchor and commuted to shore in the dinghy, a quiet cruise or a roller-coaster ride depending on the ground swell from the Atlantic. Once onshore it was bushwhacking time. The first clearing project was the entrance drive: three hundred feet from road to building site. Two

Haitian men living in the village specialized in clearing bush (the Bahamians on Crooked don't do this kind of work) but they were fully booked by folks from the village and the nearby inn. We had counted on several days of help from them, but we were on our own. The vast expanse of what I call "terminal green" was daunting, but we approached it like we'd learned to approach each phase of this project, one bush at a time.

People who build homes and live in the Seahorse Shores development are known as the "folks on the sand," because sand is indeed all there is. The downside of this is poor soil for agriculture; the upside is that most of the bush can be easily pulled from the ground with a sharp yank. We removed all but the largest trees this way then heaped them into huge burn piles. The heavy branches of the bigger shrubs and trees we dispatched with a bow saw, then hacked the roots with an ax.

Poisonwood trees required special care, especially since we were exposed to the sap from severed roots and limbs. The Haitians were expert gardeners, able to deftly remove poisonwood —we sorely missed their help. Mari and I, dressed in white disposable painter's coveralls and latex gloves, sweated off pounds while carefully hacking and stacking the branches for burning. Still, there was no avoiding the occasional outbreak. Soon we were smearing affected skin with crushed gum elemi tree leaves to help neutralize the itching and burning, quickly learning to tell the difference between the antidote and its nearly identical toxic cousin.

Working in the bush with little wind or shade turned the sun into a bully. We chugged gallons of Gatorade. Halfway through the first day we'd cleared about fifty feet of drive and Mari asked, "Is this the fun part?"

I tossed another plant on the pile. "Wait 'til we start hauling rocks." We didn't yet know about shoveling sand.

Fresh water, or lack of it, became an issue. We were both tiring of the boat routine of salt-water baths with a light fresh-water rinse. We wanted a *real* shower. The neighbors had wells ranging in depths from ten to twenty-three feet. I prayed ours would be closer to ten. I chose a favorable spot for a well and began a 5-ft. x 5-ft. excavation. It was easy enough to shovel out the first few feet of sand, but then I hit sandstone. Even the pickaxe had a tendency to bounce off the surface if the swing was less than vertical. This was turning into real one-foot-per-day stuff. I thought about the vine-shrouded backhoe I'd seen in the village and mourned its passing. But that evening, while Mari and I commiserated about the sandstone, salvation dropped anchor beside us.

Josh, 22, was from Wolf Island, Canada, and beginning a world circumnavigation aboard his 32-ft. junk-rigged sailboat, *Lorca*. His father, Dale, had joined him for the Caribbean leg of the journey. At 6'2" Josh was all muscle and, boat-bound for several weeks, craved exercise. We cut a deal for two day's work.

After two days of pick slinging, Josh was down to eight feet. It had become a personal challenge for him to strike water, and early the following day fresh water pooled at the bottom of the nine-foot hole. We'd been told that to go much deeper would be a mistake, since the fresh water floats in a thin layer atop the salt water. Dig too deep and the well turns brackish. We took it down another foot and called it a well. (Thanks again, Josh.)

My jubilation lasted until the next day when I happened to sight down our property line from a high point on the bluff. We'd sunk the well in the adjoining lot—especially embarrassing since we'd laughed at the stories about houses and garages built on the wrong lots. If the lot owners next to us ever decide to build, we'll have already contributed a house-warming gift.

A week passed and our land was now dotted with smoldering mounds of ash. We set up the canvas garage, installed the composting toilet and a pressurized outdoor shower. And finally (hooray!) the Haitian gardeners arrived in time to help clear the house site, which included two massive poisonwood trees towering in the middle of the roped-off grid. Crouching low with wide machetes, Joseph and his brother deftly jabbed and twisted, popping plants loose from their roots. Behind them, only sand remained. We'd been forewarned to carefully mark the area we wanted cleared, or risk having the entire lot turned into a desert.

Mari went around with the two expert bushwhackers and tied orange ribbon around each tree we didn't want harmed. She made an impression on those guys. When I went to remove a tree that had mistakenly been tagged Joseph yelled, "No no, the missus say no cut!" I wasn't allowed to touch it until Mari gave the okay. By 4 p.m. that day we had two monster burn piles where the house would one day stand.

In the beginning, I wasn't at all sure how being engulfed in a thicket of Crooked Island's "terminal green" would feel. But except for giant palmetto bugs (a gift-wrapped name for FCUS's: Flying Cockroaches of Unusual Size), a few feral cats and hulking blue land crabs, being in the bush was like exploring a giant terrarium. Tropical trees and flowering shrubs competed for space with scrubbier low-profile relatives. Where we didn't have to completely clear an area it felt more like a thinning a wildly overgrown garden. After a rain, the air smelled like baby powder.

We searched for the source and found a shrub dotted with clusters of tiny white blossoms.

June McMillan had a collection of dog-eared botanical reference books collected over the thirty years she and Don had wintered on Crooked. From these we began to learn the names and personality traits of some of the plants that comprised our natural landscape. Seven-year apple. Star sedge, monkey fiddle and devil's pumpkin. Sea grape, flowering almond.

Many were credited with medicinal benefits. According to one source, periwinkle rosea was used to treat ailments ranging from polio to leukemia. The invasive and prolific vine cassytha filiformis, or love vine, went after prickly heat and backache. Its other more popular use was directly related to its colloquial name.

We cleared a spot for the banana tree suckers we'd been given on Long Island. Alongside went the lime and orange saplings. June graciously wished us luck with the fledgling nursery; she'd spent years trying to get citrus to grow on their property. She'd finally taken their one surviving grapefruit tree to a friend's inland farm where it flourished in richer soil and away from salt spray.

Bird life was abundant, diverse and blessedly distracting. Our work was supervised by dozens of bananaquits, their high, hissing squeaks and buzzes sounded mechanical next to the mockingbird's aria. Ospreys often glided overhead with the daily catch still wiggling in their talons. Early mornings on the salt pond, I saw high-stepping egrets, great blue herons and occasionally, breathtakingly, the blush of flamingos.

Our terrarium was patrolled by its own stinging defense force: small, dense and militant mosquitos. The bites never itched very long, but the whine of bloodthirsty squadrons searching for undefended flesh induced bouts of shrieking, swatting hysteria.

When the wind died, the sand flies came to life. They were no bigger than a speck of pepper, but came equipped with an over-sized proboscis capable of sucking forty-five times their body weight in (my) blood. Each direct hit raised a welt that itched for days. Somewhere there is a sanitarium that houses formerly sane people who babble mindlessly while swatting at invisible intruders. They're the ones who came to the tropics without long pants, long-sleeved shirts and a return ticket.

Crooked Island had snakes, but none were poisonous. It was free of poison ivy and poison oak. But (big but) there was of course poisonwood, which trumped both its lesser genus-mates.

Still, as we hacked, sweated and scratched, the property began to open and receive us. Some measure of progress was evident by the end of each day, though the prospect of rowing to the boat after hours of bushwhacking began to rapidly lose its appeal. If it ever had any.

For Fritz it was second nature, but I still struggled with maneuvering the dinghy. It didn't just have a mind of its own, it had attitude. Timing the launch as well as disembarking meant anticipating how big, how hard and how fast the waves would break. If I was tired or dressed in anything other than disgusting work clothes, the waves would be high and the landing wet. I could count on it.

It seemed the ocean was always up to something. It was December after all, and the northeast trade winds were, as they say, blowing like stink. The resulting chop kept *San Diego* vulnerable to all kinds of hijinks, like shifting cargo and fouled anchor lines. Despite Fritz's skillfully set anchors, no boat is immune to sailing off sans crew. And a boat on the beach is like a fighter in the ring with both hands tied behind her back. Every wave lands a solid punch until there's nothing left but broken parts and disappointment.

As yet we had no onshore electricity except for a small generator—not enough to run the freezer we'd brought, stocked with food. On the trip out, the engine ran enough hours during the day to keep the inverter charged, the electricity flowing, the freezer freezing. But now the boat was in long-term parking. The only electricity being generated was from solar panels atop the cabin, and like the generator, it was not enough to supply the freezer.

So every other day, we'd fire up *San Diego's* engine for several hours to give the inverter its fix, shattering the quiet (unless the wind was louder) with the lilting melody of a diesel engine. If a cold front moved in, making the anchorage too wild for even exhausted bushwhackers to tolerate, we moved the boat to the west side and repeated the performance. I don't remember any standing ovations from our new neighbors. I do recall a comment having to do with bows, arrows and *San Diego's* target-yellow hull.

Chapter 8

Dagwood

Two weeks after we arrived, Mari and I were rowing ashore when I noticed a small gray freighter on approach to Landrail Point. She had a drunken list to port and streaks of rust trailing from her scuppers like mascara on an old trollop in tears.

I pointed. "You don't suppose that's the mailboat, do you?"

She nodded. "I heard it left Nassau yesterday."

I picked up my rowing pace. Our truck was on that boat. Before leaving Nassau we'd placed a tarp and plenty of line on the truck's front seat along with instructions for the dealer. We wanted to make sure it was covered for the salty trip to Crooked.

We arrived at the dock just as the *Lady Rosalind* lowered her ramp. And there, nestled between two containers was our little white truck. No tarp, though it seemed the containers had kept most of the salt water at bay. The tarp and line were still on the front seat. The boat's first mate drove it onto the jetty and parked. He held the keys in one hand.

He said, "You get these when we get $250."

This was $100 more than we'd been quoted for the delivery. I went to find the agent who listened to my story, then stormed aboard. We heard shouting from the bridge and eventually the agent returned with a dubious compromise. "They'll take two hundred dollars. I can't get it no better." Stuck, we paid it. Later, when we heard the *Lady Rosalind* ran afoul of Hogsty Reef on her way to Great Inagua we silently saluted the power of karma.

We were proud of our Tonka-toy look-alike flatbed. With graphically placed black electrical tape, we changed the name on the tailgate from DAEWOO to DAGWOOD.

Enter Martin, a heavy-equipment driver from Nassau who, lacking other transportation, drove the Caterpillar payloader he operated like anyone else would drive a car, including bar-hopping from village to village. At night. Drunk.

A week after receiving the truck we loaned it to a neighbor, Woody, to haul some friends into the village for dinner. We later followed with Doug and Christel in their station wagon. As we approached Landrail Point's main intersection, we spotted Dagwood parked in the middle of the road.

Immediately speculating as to why Woody would park the truck there, we noticed a crowd had gathered, Martin staggering among them. Fifty yards down the road in front of Gibson's Lunchroom was the massive yellow payloader. Which was where Dagwood had been parked when Martin came careening down the street, bucket down, and smacked into the front of it. At first glance the truck looked fine, but it was dark outside. Looking closer, I saw a deep cleft in the driver's side corner post where the impact occurred. The door and window were also somewhat askew. No broken lights. The windshield was intact. How had this little truck survived the Battle of the Payloader?

Woody had unintentionally left the truck in neutral without the parking brake on. As a result, Dagwood recoiled from the payloader's impact and rolled down the road with minimal damage. Nobody volunteered to claim responsibility. Martin, with a drunken swagger, began to give Mari an "interfering white folks" rant, but others in the group cooled him off.

Instead of contacting the police, a local man quietly placed a call to Martin's employer in Nassau who flew to Crooked the next day. Meanwhile, we drove the truck to Max, Crooked Island's only body shop man, who said he'd fix the damage for three hundred dollars. Later we were summoned to a house in Landrail to meet with Martin's boss, dressed head to toe in white Nike tennis apparel. He calmly apologized for his employee's behavior while peeling crisp $100 bills from a stuffed wallet. He hesitated at five and asked if that would be sufficient. We said yes.

Let me guess. You're wondering what happened to the moonlit beach walks, the boating excursions, the snorkeling, the long, lazy days. They haven't disappeared. They're still here, still available, still being enjoyed—by people on vacation. Which now, were not us.

When we traded our tourist's sarongs for homebuilder's coveralls, we crossed that invisible, powerful boundary that separates paradise from real life. It didn't matter where in the world we were. It could have been a mountain cabin or Provençal village, New York City or New Zealand. For us, it just happened to be a ninety square-mile limestone protrusion surrounded by water.

From the beginning, it was clear it would be tricky to negotiate the line between magical and menial. If we allowed ourselves to get completely lost in the day-to-day, we would accomplish nothing more than a location and career change (with a 100% pay cut). So far this new life had created a vacuum where tension and stress used to live, but it could easily fill again.

Playing a sleepy game of Scrabble one night I removed one vowel, slightly shifted the letters and the word exotic became toxic.

Next morning, a few notes of a familiar tune jingled in the background of a VHF radio transmission. Without the usual reminders, I'd forgotten the holiday was approaching. I fed branches into a pile of burning brush and remembered Libby, a friend I had when I was growing up in northern Illinois. Each winter Libby's parents carted her off to California for Christmas. One year she brought back a photo of her aunt's suburban Los Angeles split level, decorated for the holidays.

The house was white with a red tile roof. No snow. Not even grass. Plastic snowmen were stuck in the sand on either side of the front door. Santa stood next to his sleigh near the edge of the roof, one arm raised in a wave, the other clutching a bag of presents. Two of the reindeer were prone, though Rudolf still cheerfully, permanently pranced.

Baby Jesus lay under a coconut palm in the front yard, surrounded by the usual suspects. Libby stood between the snowmen, hands clenched at her side, smiling the kind of smile reserved for family reunions and church directory photos.

There were some serious issues here. Where was the snow? What was Santa doing on a roof with no chimney? How could they mix the church part of Christmas with the Santa part? Someone needed to tell these Californians the rules: Frosty, Rudolf and Santa were on one side of the Christmas tracks, the Virgin Mary, Jesus and three wise men on the other.

Despite inevitable changes in family and habitat, for the next fifteen years I adhered like a soldier to traditional holiday celebrations. When my son was born the rituals took on new meaning. No question about it, I was a Norman Rockwell Christmas poster child. But not for long.

The first challenge to what I thought was my impenetrable holiday defense came when Seth was five. Somehow on December 25th, we found ourselves not in Stockbridge, Massachusetts, or even Whitewater, Wisconsin, but in a faux-abode townhouse in Albuquerque, New Mexico. I braced myself, but what I thought would be a debacle worthy of its own tragic snapshot was instead enchanting. True, the only snow visible was draped over the crest of the Sandia Mountains, far above the city. And the air temperature was decidedly warmer than could be entirely proper for December.

It was the luminarias (votive candles nested in paper sacks), the sweet biscochitos and chili-laden posole—the entire fragrant, edible Hispanic tradition of Christmas that won me over. I now realize that for me, New Mexico was holiday halfway house. Because, after twenty years of red chili lights and tamales, a Crooked Island Christmas loomed.

The Bahamas gained independence from Great Britain in 1973, but three centuries of English influence doesn't evaporate overnight. We drive on the left, refer to police officers as constables and get our butter from New Zealand, another British Commonwealth country. I imagine in Nassau, the remaining English gentry still commemorate Christmas with Dickensian flair. Figgy pudding? Plum tarts? But by the time Christmas has weathered the long voyage to the out-islands, all this has been considerably diluted.

Holiday adornment in Landrail Point was a half-melted red candle nested in plastic holly on the table at Gibson's Lunchroom.

I counted down the days not with partridges in pear trees, but mosquitoes in poisonwood. I recalled Libby's photo and realized I was in it.

But then Josh and Dale anchored next to us, and Josh began helping with the well. Josh's mom flew in from Canada to spend the holiday with her family. June and Don invited all of us for turkey on Christmas Eve. Next morning the Seventh Day Adventist church in Landrail rocked Hallelujahs and rolled Praise the Lords. Santa swapped his sleigh for a Cessna 172 and touched down at the landing strip with a bag full of gifts for the village kids.

At noon, as she had for the previous thirty years, Marina Gibson prepared lunch for the entire community and served it under a spreading mamey tree in the restaurant's courtyard. People we knew and people we'd just met laughed, talked and feasted on grouper, snapper, mac & cheese, coleslaw, peas 'n rice. Later that afternoon, Fritz pulled on fins, mask and snorkel and disappeared into the water, spear in hand. When he returned we dug a pit in the sand on the beach, built a fire and let it burn down to coals. On top of the coals we placed, wrapped in foil and drenched in butter, the tail from the biggest lobster I'd ever seen. It slow-roasted while the sun set through a swath of greens and blues shot through with orange.

There's a photo of me sitting in the sand, leaning against a coconut palm, balancing a paper plate on my lap. I'm smiling the kind of smile reserved for someone eating lobster on Christmas Day. I wish Libby could see it.

Chapter 9
Sand, Barge & Beyond

Finally, the fun part. Staking out dimensions and elevations for the house revealed just how it would sit on the property, also how to maximize the view as well as take advantage of prevailing winds. The outer dimensions were 32' wide and 28' deep, the lower level half that.

The fun lasted until I realized how deep the excavation would need to be to accommodate the split-level design. Before the site was cleared, the slope looked far steeper than the true measurements. My eyeball had really missed the target this time; the booby prize was fifty cubic yards of extra sand. I briefly considered scrapping the split-level idea, but a new plan would have required entirely different materials and ours were already on the way.

Getting rid of the sand became a priority—we couldn't dig the footings until it was gone. Again I wept over the fate of that backhoe.

We used a few future floor joists to make a ramp to the top of the bluff. With a load of exactly twenty-four shovelfuls of sand, we ran a wheelbarrow up the hill—walking didn't work—then dumped the load onto the beach. Then did it again. And again. And again. Josh gave us a couple more days of help and we also tried to recruit Joseph and Joel. "Yes, we come check you, yes," they always responded, but never appeared.

A long week later we had shifted every last grain. We saw Joseph on the road and using our poor French tried to explain that we no longer needed his help. He nodded and smiled. "Okay, okay."

Not long after, we took an early walk down the beach to visit the McMillans. Don took a puff from his cigar and mentioned he'd seen one of the Haitians bicycle past a half-hour earlier. There were several other homes beyond the McMillan's, but Mari and I were the only ones currently around. We looked at each other and bolted for the door.

We jogged the quarter-mile to our drive and there was the human brush-hog, energetically denuding our yard. He'd already cleared twenty feet of bush back from the road. I can't imagine what he thought of the two hysterical white people yelling "No no no, enough, enough, enough. Thank you, *merci,* thank you!" I thrust a twenty in his hand and as politely as I could, shooed him down the road.

The quality of the sand proved ideal for trenching the foundation and column footings, just stiff enough to hold its shape but soft enough to dig with very light foot pressure. In this way the sand could be used as molds for all the foundation work.

Now all we needed was concrete. And for that we needed the barge.

Late by almost two weeks, we watched through binoculars as the *MV Cavalier* arrived, vanishing under spectacular sheets of white spray whenever an extra large wave slammed against the hull. The closer it came, the more it showed evidence of a hard journey and heavy seas. Loose tendrils of shrink-wrap flailed in the wind, stacks of lumber tilted askew. Oddly, the two 45-foot containers that held ours and neighbor Bruce's supplies were parked under the relative protection of the superstructure. And it looked like all the lumber and sacks of concrete mix were stacked on the exposed deck.

Any barge landing is a major community affair, and all agreed they had never seen one so heavily laden. Once the ramp was down and the first truckload of lumber rolled off, we boarded the vessel to inspect the goods.

The water on deck had at times been two feet deep. The first two layers of shrink-wrapped concrete mix on each pallet were soaked; sixteen bags per pallet would soon be stone. Water still dribbled from the bundles of the pine tongue-and-groove planks destined for our floor and roof. Since all this wood and concrete mix should have been protected in the container, and was in fact one of the major reasons we *bought* a container, what exactly, we asked ourselves, was in it?

When we finally opened the doors, it was virtually empty except for appliances, metal roofing, two pallets of concrete patio pavers and two thousand-gallon plastic cistern tanks. Outdoor pavers. Plastic tanks. Sure wouldn't have wanted those to get wet now, would we? Even more disheartening was the absence of our patio door and all the windows (Re: Expensive Lesson #4: *Pack Your Own Container.*)

Crooked Island is not a Bahamian port of entry. To clear the barge the group had to fly in and pay overtime charges for two customs agents from Georgetown, Exuma. The customs broker in Nassau had yet to fax the necessary paperwork, but a barrage of irate phone calls got her motivated and the papers arrived by late afternoon. Meanwhile, our expensive customs agents snoozed under a palm tree when they weren't hunting crabs.

As agreed, Cooter provided a flatbed trailer and all-terrain forklift to move the materials to their respective building sites. A man named Calvin was the flatbed's designated driver. Calvin was upset about missing a televised Miami Dolphins game and fumed at the many delays, most caused by his own reckless driving. Bruce and I took turns driving the forklift, spending more time pulling Calvin and the truck from the sand than unloading materials.

Eventually we discovered that beer kept Calvin on the manic side of manic/depressive, so we set up watering holes along the three-mile long road leading to the building sites. Timing it carefully, one of us would thrust a cold one into Calvin's outstretched hand as he drove by. He may have been a hazardous driver, but he never missed a hand-off. Although now when he got stuck, he got *really* stuck. We added a chain saw to the extrication arsenal.

By evening of the second day the barge was empty, but there was still a third of the load on the jetty. A cold front was approaching and the barge skipper was anxious about his exposed mooring. If given the chance, we suspected he'd sneak away that night. With our building sites three miles from the harbor, what remained would require weeks of manhandling and trips in our truck. We waited until the day's last load was delivered then hid the forklift in the bush to insure the skipper's compliance. After the way our goods had been handled we were showing no mercy.

Next morning, no cold front. Eventually Calvin got lubricated enough to roar off with another load. Returning to the jetty, a large hydraulic ram used to manipulate the trailer hitch snapped off and plowed up a half-mile of roadbed. I spent thirty minutes under the truck and managed to remove the entire thing. The trick was to make sure the trailer wasn't detached before we were finished and that meant keeping Calvin happy, an increasingly difficult task. In fact, having had their fill of mosquitoes (or, actually, vise versa), bossy landowners and no television, the skipper and Calvin had conspired to shut down the operation while I worked on the truck. With one major load yet to be dispersed Calvin drove past me, this time not to the jetty but directly onto the barge, forklift in tow. Before we could do anything more than yell, the loading ramp closed and the barge pulled away.

A stack of sheetrock was all that remained on the jetty for Mari and me—three truckloads later it was onsite. Not so Bruce, who had to commission the inn's big flatbed and hire some local muscle to move the remainder of his lumber and concrete-block, an expensive two-day effort.

At midnight on New Year's Eve, under a full moon, Josh hoisted Lorca's red sail and set a course to Cuba, his next destination. His dad planned to stay with him for several more weeks before returning home to Canada. After that, Josh was on his own.

It was like saying goodbye to a favorite nephew. I began to understand how relationships could be so quickly formed between travelers far away from the familiar. Even though Fritz and I intended to sink roots here, our connection was still tenuous—we didn't yet know if it would take hold and thrive. By sharing some of the shoveling, sweating, complaining and laughing, Josh had contributed more than youthful ebullience to our project. Like others who helped during those early days, his enthusiasm broadened the experience, repeatedly hoisting it out of isolation and into community.

Sailing his sloop alongside *Lorca* for the next leg of the journey was Glen, a crusty Canadian friend of Don and June's who'd recently surfaced after having been feared lost at sea. No one had seen nor heard from him in many months so his family finally conducted a memorial service. Glen's response to all the fuss? "I wasn't lost. I always knew where I was." (Before Glen sailed, Fritz shimmied up his boat's mast to repair some rigging, something Glen could no longer manage. Later Glen delivered a bottle of rum along with an admonishment: "This doesn't mean I like you.")

We stood on the moonlit beach until the boats became dots on the luminous horizon, then said a final Happy New Year to the assembled group and headed for our dinghy. The row out to *San Diego* was quiet, but during the night the wind increased from ten to twenty-five knots. I spent another night observing Fritz sleep like a baby being rocked in a cradle.

Next morning, groggy and struggling for balance, I reached for a bowl, one that Fritz's sister Carla, a potter, had made. I managed to fill it then steadied myself on the edge of the sink before attempting a spoonful. Just then a wave slammed into the hull and a grapefruit shot like a cannon out of a net overhead. It whacked me on the head before landing in the middle of the full bowl, which burst into shards, spraying the cabin with milk and cereal.

Fritz stepped into the cabin and took one look at the scene before pivoting smartly and stepping back out on deck. It's a good thing I didn't get a look at his face.

Chapter 10
Concrete

Eleven hundred sacks of cement stacked on twenty-one wooden pallets surrounded the building site. Over the next weeks and months, the pyramids would shrink as they were hoisted into the mixer, two sacks at a time. For now, the piles taunted us with their mass.

The re-bar, drenched with saltwater on the barge, began corroding. We attacked the flaky rust with wire brushes and treated each 20' length with an agent containing phosphoric acid to halt the oxidation. Next time: galvanized re-bar.

After a rolling breakfast aboard *San Diego* followed by the row ashore, our workdays began when I yanked the starter cord on the portable generator. It sputtered and roared to life, pumping out a whopping 1500 watts of 110-volt juice. The electric cement mixer pulsed with a grinding three/four beat that would be our background music for the next four months. We set re-bar, oiled the wooden molds, then either poured a section of foundation or framed-up another column.

Mari used a three-step procedure to dump the 60 lb. sacks of concrete into the mixer. One: Open bag and lift to hip. Two: Free-jerk to shoulder. Three: Jettison contents over lip of mixer. After three weeks, she had honed the exercise to one swift move—rip-lift-dump.

Nobody messed with Mari.

Re-bar in place, the mixer churned out a wheelbarrow-load of cement every ten minutes and the trenched footings slowly took shape. Empty brown sacks began to accumulate.

Don and June dropped by several times a week. While Don relieved Mari at the mixer—I was the wheelbarrow guy—June poured coffee from a thermos and passed the muffins. If, for whatever reason, time spread out between visits, I'd get downright grumpy. Those visits (especially the muffins) took the bite out of the heat and mosquitoes.

In the boating world, Crooked's anchorage was politely called animated. In other words, uncomfortable. There are no calm or protected anchorages on the north end of Crooked Island. With the prevailing winds from the east, the sandy bight on the west side was relatively flat; without the radical roll of the north shore we could usually get a decent night's sleep. However, when the wind shifted, look out!

At 4 a.m. one morning a huge groundswell moved in, the result of a heavy blow in the North Atlantic. We woke up to *San Diego* bucking in breaking surf. With each thunderous roll of a wave her bow lurched skyward and the anchors dragged another foot or two in the fine white sand. The beach was only yards away when I got the engine fired up. With Mari at the helm we managed to retrieve both anchors and power through the surf into open ocean—all this while naked with several telescopes, we were later told, focused on the action.

Eight miles south lay the cut into French Wells, the only fully protected anchorage on Crooked Island. We arrived at dawn to a solid wall of surf across the entrance to the lagoon. We knew where the channel was so I lined her up and shot through on a big wave.

The concrete could wait. After a couple of days of spearfishing, touch-up painting and beachcombing, the ground swell had all but disappeared, as had our fatigue. We were ready for more mixing.

This time it was columns, poured in an 8"x8" bolted-together form that stood 8' tall. With an inner core of re-bar, each of the thirteen columns took seven sacks of concrete. I positioned myself five rungs high on the ladder, Mari hoisted a bucket of cement and I dumped it in. We could only pour one column each day, which left plenty of time to scour the island for rock.

Our previous home had been built of cinderblock and neither of us wanted another block home. We opted to use this concrete version of post and beam construction and fill all the open space between columns and window frames with native limestone and coral rock. Now, twenty Dagwood-loads later, piles of rock competed for space with the stacks of concrete surrounding the building site.

Woody and Shirley Lippincott aren't marriage counselors, but they could be. They had just finished building a sturdy, stuccoed house a quarter-mile down the beach from us. As busy Miami-based professionals, they couldn't visit the Island for more than a few weeks each year. After spending the holidays on Crooked, the Lippincotts left in early January, but a month later sent word with island-bound friends that they were interested in having us stay in their house. It was too much trouble, they said, to completely open, then close the house each time they came for a short visit. Also, houses and yards, especially in salt-water environments, fare better when faucets are regularly opened, toilets flushed, burr-grass pulled. If we wouldn't mind moving back onto the boat during the limited times they were there, they'd appreciate it if we looked after the place.

I am not normally an expeditious packer, but that day I grabbed a bag, stuffed in some clothes and toiletries and levitated ashore. I took a shower with warm water. I baked a pizza for supper and never once clutched the counter or ducked a falling citrus. Later, sitting in Adirondack-style chairs on the front deck, Fritz and I watched pinpoints of stars appear and multiply. I checked the position of recognizable constellations to see if anything was aligned differently. Sleep was deep that night; dreams had already come true.

Chapter 11

Lifeline

Since colonial days, the mailboat has been the lifeline of the Bahamas, relied upon for the necessities, and a few frills, of life. The structure that now houses Pittstown Point Landing's kitchen was originally the first Bahamian post office. The hand-hewn blocks of sandstone, cemented in place by early 19th-century craftsmen, have weathered many storms. And so have the boats that delivered the mail.

The Crooked Island Passage is the safest deep-water route through The Bahamas. For centuries, ships from around the world have sailed or steamed around the northwest corner of Crooked Island on their way to or from Panama or the Gulf of Mexico, trading news and cargo from abroad. From Crooked, smaller fleets of trading vessels distributed mail and cargo throughout the chain of seven hundred islands that comprise The Bahamas.

When Nassau, New Providence, became both the capital and primary clearing-house for imported goods, the government contracted specific boats to carry mail and cargo to the out-islands. An organized distribution network began to take shape. Until the late 1940s, Crooked's mailboat was powered by sail alone. Back then its arrival was, at best, a monthly occurrence, often every two months.

On board were staples, like rice and other dry-goods (rarely dry), building materials and mail. No one expected fresh produce;

it was strictly "grow your own." Passengers traveled at their own risk, as did captain and crew.

In our island neighborhood, mailboat stories rivaled lost-at-sea stories.

In 1975, I sailed into Clarencetown, Long Island, and met the one-legged man who'd been captain of their previous mailboat. He'd cut his leg on a coral reef while trying to dislodge the mailboat. He freed the boat but wasn't able to prevent the ensuing infection.

An older Crooked Islander told me of a time when the mailboat hadn't come in nearly four months. Desperate, he and another man rowed out into the Crooked Island Passage to flag a passing freighter and beg for food. Their bold move paid off; they returned with sacks of flour, sugar and tinned stew.

Mailboat Day is a social event, as is Airplane Day and (as we'd just witnessed) Barge Day. Crowds are expected. *Lady Matilda* arrived late one afternoon and tied alongside the town jetty. A substantial swell weaseled its way in from the north, adding a slow roll to her deck. *Lady Matilda* was the first boat in two weeks, so not only was the crowd large, it was eager.

Her decks were crammed with cars, boats and heavy equipment destined for points south. The side-mounted crane was being used to shift the heavy, palletized cargo from the hold; unloading would carry on well into the night. All items under a hundred pounds—cases of beer, soft drinks, tires, flour, etc.—were a toss and catch affair, timed with the roll of the deck.

We arrived after dark and there was already a hip-high wall of cargo piled on the jetty. Surrounding the booty were thirty or forty eager recipients searching for packages bearing their names. The crane operator, one hand on the controls and one hand around a bottle of Kalik beer, was shouting something to the crew in the hold.

Tension tightened the crane cables and a yellow forklift rose out of the hold. The strain on the hydraulic pump was clearly audible. As it cleared the deck hatch, wave action was transmitted to the top of the crane and the forklift took on a life of its own. Each roll of the deck increased the arc of its swing until the forks were twirling like the horns of an enraged bull.

The crane operator dropped his beer and grabbed for the controls.

The forklift's first casualty was the canvas T-top of a sport-fishing boat. The forks hung up briefly on the frame after shredding the canvas, while deck hands scrambled to lasso the swinging ton of compact metal. All eyes on shore followed the beast's ever increasing motion. The crane operator tried to lower the load but it only widened the arc and exaggerated the swing.

The next victim was the stainless steel frame holding the now shredded canvas T-top. A wrenching clash of metal left a twisted mass of shiny tubes and the yellow bull swung back across the deck in a wild spin. Momentum had now increased the arc to over fifty feet. The forklift once again swung toward the jetty, this time clearing the deck cargo. At the top of the arc the crane operator released the cable brake and the forklift flew onto the jetty.

I yelled, "Holy shit!"

Mari and I and the rest of the crowd dove for cover in a confusion of arms, legs and dust. The forklift cut a swath through the wall of cargo and thumped to the ground. There was not one sound for thirty seconds and then we all burst out laughing.

Chapter 12
Prune Juice

I stood just inside the sliding glass door of Landrail Point's only food store and peered down at a soggy cardboard box marked Chiquita. The mailboat had just pulled away from the island and I'd holstered my machete long enough to race into the settlement before all the fresh produce disappeared. (Unlike my neighbors, I had still had plenty of eggs. Note to skeptics: coating eggs with Vaseline actually works.) Owner Daisy Scavella was busy behind the counter, tallying the prices of someone's grocery items. Potatoes, then onions and cassava were weighed in a rusty scale that hung from the ceiling. The amount was written in a notebook, then totaled.

I wondered how long it had taken the bananas inside the box to journey from green, to ripe, to completely black. At some point, a long, long time ago, each one of them had reached its moment of perfect ripeness. But no one had been there to witness it, let alone peel and savor. Now, like deliveries from the previous two mailboats, they were beyond even banana bread stage. There was only one word for what I saw: compost.

It suddenly reminded me of the reverence in Christel's eyes when she unpacked the fruit and vegetables we'd brought along on our first visit. Call it clouded hindsight or potassium deficiency, but the only time I'd seen a similar look it had been worn by a film actor who'd just been handed a cup of water after surviving a ten-day trek across the desert.

Skunked out of bananas for another week, I squeezed between several equally disappointed neighbors to scrounge for consolation produce. It took five steps to walk the length of the east aisle (corned-beef hash to sugar), three steps to cross the south end (grits to hot sauce), five steps to return to GO (instant yeast to hair tonic). Stacked on the floor near the checkout counter was a large sack of raw peanuts and a box each of onions, potatoes and sweet potatoes. (Bahamian sweet potatoes are often a white-fleshed, starchier version of the pumpkin-tinted American variety.) There were a few cassavas, plantains and some small, wilted cabbages.

I wasn't sure what to do with cassava, so I grabbed two plantains and a cabbage, weighed them and waited until Miss Daisy was ready to check me out. I wanted to ask if she still had to pay for the produce that arrived in such sorry, smelly condition, but she was a quiet woman I didn't yet know well. She'd lost her husband in an airplane crash several years before and she moved and spoke with an elegant reserve that felt impenetrable. I thanked her and drove to the property, resolved to do whatever it took to coax my garden and our fledgling banana and lime trees into productivity.

I'd cleared a space for a vegetable garden behind the house site that I thought would provide wind-protection, yet not be so far in the bush that I hadn't a prayer of surviving mosquito attacks. Getting seeds to sprout was easy, but the loose, sandy mixture we referred to as soil held few of the nutrients needed to sustain growth. Fertilizing was like ringing a dinner bell for hungry roots from the surrounding bush. Water seemed to evaporate before it reached the sand, plus mixing concrete was already placing big demands on our new well. We didn't have much water to spare.

But it was the crabs that had me stumped. In the garden every morning there were newly excavated piles of sand, as if a dozen miniature volcanoes had erupted. If I smoothed and reseeded the area, a new hole waited, triumphant, the next morning. I finally floated my problem on the island grapevine and reeled in a tip.

Nicker beans live inside a large, prickly pod on a bush covered with barbed thorns. When the pods mature they split and the beans fall to the ground where they can be retrieved with minimal blood loss. They're the size of a marble or plump lima bean, and unlike their host plant, are smooth and friendly.

You can't imagine how much fun it was to roll a nicker bean down a crab hole. Whatever the reason, crabs were flummoxed by the appearance of a bean in a tunnel. Rather than dig new ones, most eventually crawled to a friendlier neighborhood. Only a few more intellectually precocious crabs stuck around to see if fate could be altered. They were the ones who, each night, rolled the beans back up out of the holes. It was kind of like playing a really, really slow game of croquet, without mallets or wickets. Also, my opponent and I kept scoring the same point, over and over. So far, my career total was seven consecutive bean-in, bean-out exchanges. But it was early in the season.

Until my garden grew, we relied on occasional inland sources of citrus, supplemented with fresh produce generously flown in by neighbors and visitors. Sometimes it was even possible to place special orders, though scratchy phone lines often caused confusion. After a particularly dry stretch, June McMillan asked incoming friends to simply bring "produce." Questioning her order must have seemed indelicate, so several days later a case of prune juice was quietly left at her door.

Chapter 13
Miss Connie

Within days of moving into Woody and Shirley's house, Marina sent a message that my mother would call that evening. Even though every few weeks we'd go through the process of reassuring both our families, it hadn't been that long since Connie and I had last spoken. The premonition demons were set loose; I worked through every worse case scenario the four-hour wait allowed. When I arrived at Gibson's Lunchroom, Marina handed me an iced tea while I chatted with a couple of visiting yachties and waited for my call.

Considering the equipment's lack of sophistication and its rudimentary installation, I was always amazed when the phone actually rang. Between echoes and voice delays—it was more like a conversation in code—my mother got her message across. She'd already booked tickets for Crooked Island. The good news was she wouldn't have to stay on the boat.

Unlike some older parents, Connie was still a mover and a shaker. She had always encouraged my wanderings and I soon understood that it gave her an excuse to travel. I knew she'd be an asset to our project as long as I could keep her delegated.

When she arrived the following week we had just begun laying rocks for the lower walls of the house. This was a process that would extend well beyond her visit and made delegating mom-labor a snap. Connie became our official chinker, responsible for fitting the small bits that would fill any gaps between larger rocks. Each day she rummaged through piles of rock to find appropriately sized and shaped shells and coral pieces. Working in the shade of our makeshift awning, she eventually had her personal mound of chinkers and was kept busy filling all the odd spaces as the walls rose.

Whenever the over-the-shoulder commentary increased ("Are you sure that's strong enough?" or "That doesn't really look like it fits"), I knew it was time to pile on a few errands or suggest she start dinner.

One day Mari and I had business down-island. We dropped off Connie at Marina's for a visit. The two women had quickly become friends and we thought it was time to give Mom a temporary reprieve from the chinker gang. When we returned two hours later she greeted us with a terse "Where have you been?"

Connie didn't yet understand about island time, but would soon enough. This visit was only the beginning of my mother's experience with Crooked Island. Already she was meeting people and making connections. On our way to the village for dinner one evening we drove past a group of local teenagers and heard them call, "Hello, Miss Connie!"

I looked at Mari and she just smiled and shrugged.

The two weeks shot by. We took time to hit island highlights even as work progressed. Connie was a great help—the section of wall she worked on was the best chinked of all—but it's always nice to get your space back. A couple of days after she returned to the States she called to let us know she was home safe and sound, then announced, "I need a beach and an ocean in my life. What would you think if I moved to Crooked Island?"

Rarely am I speechless.

I might have first started liking my mother-in-law because she liked me, but before long I fell for Connie because I'd never, ever met anyone quite like her. In my Midwestern neck of the woods, women of my mother's generation specialized in casseroles, ironing and church picnics. Even though Connie was born in Oshkosh, Wisconsin, and made a mean vegetable lasagna, the similarity ended there.

In 1944, when her father nixed the college she had chosen in favor of a "teacher's" school, Connie protested by majoring in aviation. She left her first marriage, to Fritz's dad, when she felt herself becoming a cartoon strip Blondie. She settled in New Mexico after pinning a thumbtack on a map while blindfolded, then later bought a ranch and turned it into a women's retreat center.

The first time Connie visited Crooked Island, she took one look at my sweat-stained attire, got a whiff of eau d' Off and pulled me aside. "How's he treating you?" she wanted to know.

I'm sure it helped that I'd first met her through my friendship with Carla, years before I met Fritz. We'd had a chance to get to know each other before potentially volatile in-law labels were attached. Not that it was always seamless. I never open a washing-machine lid without hearing Connie's voice as she peeked over my shoulder one day during that first visit and casually said, "That's already overloaded."

When Connie's younger son's girlfriend—an actress plugged into the Los Angeles endless beauty fantasy—offered to set up an appointment to smooth her facial wrinkles, Connie was aghast. "I earned every one of these," she said. "Why would I give them up?"

We were now three months into the house-building project; it was six months since we'd left New Mexico. Outgoing phone calls often required more patience than even I could muster. Each time I was able to get through to my mother I could hear worry seep through her attempt at cheerfulness. Once when phone connections had been spotty for weeks, I drove the twenty miles inland to the Batelco company office and sat in the outdoor booth punching numbers for an hour before finally connecting. When my mother heard my voice she burst into tears.

What exactly was I up to, after all? For twenty years, I'd been leading a life that, while some distance away, at least made sense to my family. We could frequently talk and stay involved in one another's lives. We exchanged packages every Christmas and visits most summers. Now I had dropped into a foreign void where phones didn't work and packages sent from the States were either held ransom for exorbitant duty or delivered to Bermuda instead of The Bahamas.

Even with the recent gift of land-based lodging, the cumulative physical and emotional effort of the previous six months would have begun taking a far greater toll if Connie hadn't swooped in. Like the smell and taste of comfort food, her quirky but solidly maternal energy cast a net of reassurance around me. It never occurred to her to wonder what we were doing. Or why. She'd already been down similar roads many times in her life—this was just one more interesting fork.

But did she really want to make Crooked Island her new home?

Rock by rock, shell by shell, the walls of the house grew taller and began to define both the shape and personality of the house.

We invited neighbors to contribute a rock they liked, then supplied neoprene gloves and glob of mortar mix so they could place it themselves in the wall. Only some of the exterior walls would be rocked; it would be the job of the framed portions to balance these more organic, substantial sections. In the beginning, it took many trips to the rock pile to find the next "right" piece. Some coral rocks were so beautifully shaped and colored I began shifting them off to a separate pile even if they didn't yet fit anywhere. Fritz, of course, was also hoarding his favorites. When the only stones left in the shared pile were plain, round and white, we were forced into negotiations. Reluctantly, both sides agreed to a trade agreement. It remains unsigned.

By the time we reached the ocean side of the house, we had both developed an eye for placement. Instead of three trips to the pile to find the right stone, it usually took one. Pieces locked together like a giant, three-dimensional jigsaw puzzle. Despite the heat, the mess, the lifting and hauling, I was both sad and relieved when the last piece was laid.

What would I have done differently? I would have made a map of where everyone's stones were placed.

Chapter 14

What Lies Beneath

No shopping, no golf, no resorts, no rent-a-beach-umbrellas, no paragliding, no personal watercraft rentals, no fancy dining, no umbrella drinks, no tourist centers, plenty of sand flies and mosquitoes—so what is Crooked Island's big draw?

Yes, the Caribbean's multi-hues of blue and turquoise are a feast for the eye, but don a mask and snorkel and it all becomes clear. Add a set of fins and it's time to get wet.

Under the surface, what looks like white, sandy ocean bottom with scattered dark splotches becomes a crystalline array of rainbow colors. An infinite swirl of geometric shapes bank into wavy furrows like a field plowed by a tipsy farmer. Circular sand dollars, knobs of coral and undulating purple sea fans keep me drifting for hours in a slow current.

Slender wrasse dart into sandy caves; manta rays glide by in slow motion. Blue runners and ocean triggerfish are silvery shadows in the distance. Someday—I'm sure of it—the glint of a gold doubloon will catch my eye.

Meanwhile, there's my old buddy, the ubiquitous barracuda. With his tough guy underbite and gnarly teeth, he often drifts in and out of my visual range. Barracudas are two to four feet long (magnified 20% underwater) and torpedo-shaped. They're always curious about new kids, like me, on the block. They have a startling tendency to appear when least expected, but in my experience are harmless unless tempted by sparkling jewelry, or blood.

The sea bottom is also home to the queen conch. Its thick steak of rich meat can be prepared in numerous tasty ways. Although a large football-sized shell with distinctive spikes, it can be tough to spot if partially buried or wearing a wig of seaweed. Often I'll see their distinctive double track on the sandy bottom before sighting the shell.

The big drawback to conch is cleaning them. Using a hammer, I knock a small opening on the conical top then reach in with a filet knife to slice muscle from shell. A light tug on the claw foot usually pulls the animal—a slimy mass of spiraled entrails and meat—from the shell. Like oysters, one always wonders who ate the first one. A clear, six-inch long membranous string dangles from the glob. This dubious delicacy, the conch noodle, is prized as a virility booster. I slurp it down so I can keep deleting the Viagra ads from my stateside email.

I cut most of the dangling guts free from the main body, then clean out the alimentary canal before removing the toenail-like claw. Then, slicing across the thick foot, I grip the slimy skin with the knife's edge and rip the skin loose to expose the white meat underneath. The pros do this in one swift movement but I still fumble with the process. The conch often shoots from my grip like a bar of soap before the skin is finally removed in shreds. One of our Bahamian neighbors taught me to skin the conch with my teeth, a common local practice, but Mari nixed the technique on grounds of negative kissability.

Finally, a last plunge in the ocean to scrub off the conch slime that sticks like contact cement to my wetsuit, hammer, gloves and knife, and the process is complete.

Not one to waste a good shell as doorstop, bookend or driveway liner, I've begun fashioning their spectacular pearly-pink shells into musical instruments. Conch horns deliver a clear penetrating tone that carries a great distance (some practice required) and are rumored to call mermaids from the sea. I'll get back to you on that.

Beneath the water, those dark splotches seen from shore become coral formations of mesmerizing articulation. Time evaporates in clouds of neon fish, from the dime-sized peppermint gobi to the platter-sized parrotfish that give a new twist to the color turquoise. Gently kicking with my fins, I glide through squadrons of blue tangs while negotiating the reef's canyons, keeping a wary eye for red blaze-of-fire coral. One touch delivers a burning rash that lasts for days. A Hawksbill turtle peeks out from behind a green sponge, watches for a moment, then scoots away in a panicky hurry. I soon spot him, head tucked under a coral shelf, hiding like an ostrich.

The telltale twig of an antenna beckons me downward in a shallow dive. Tucked under a low shelf is a granddaddy lobster that looks like an alien bug with its spiked protuberances and globular eyes. A quick shot with my pole spear and twang! Dinner.

On my way to shore, I spot a camo-striped Nassau grouper deep in a hole. Curiosity aroused, its cow-eyes follow my progress. There was a time I might have tracked him down for another meal, but I no longer shoot fish without a dinghy nearby.

Last year I speared a banquet-sized grouper in twenty feet of water and began to ascend. Halfway to the surface, the fish shook itself off the spear. I watched him dart back to the reef and decided to go up for a lungful of air before giving chase. At that instant I felt a hard bump to my shoulder as a six-foot long lemon shark blasted by me, lured by the blood of the injured grouper. I surfaced and realized I was at least a hundred yards from the dinghy.

Lucky on two counts. I wasn't still towing a bloody fish, and therefore, I still had an arm.

Christopher Columbus still gets credited with "discovering" the Bahamas, though it has become pretty clear that he was at least seven decades late for the ribbon cutting. Even if one ignores—like the European explorers did—the presence of an indigenous population, evidence is mounting to support a much earlier visit by a fleet of giant Chinese treasure ships. (See the book *1421, The Year The Chinese Discovered America*, by Gavin Menzies.)

Obviously, Columbus had the bigger historical impact. Even in 1492, it seems the bullies who bloodied the most noses, or in this case, decimated the largest population, got the buzz, the spoils and eventually, the signature holidays and annoying limericks.

That'll teach the Chinese to glide quietly through unknown territory with a "do no harm" mandate. Maybe if they had skewered more Lucayan Indians, demanded gold and conversion to Buddhism, the U.S. would celebrate Zhou Wen Day the second Monday of each October.

These are the things I think about while snorkeling to take my mind off sharks.

During our first (and you now know, fateful) visit to Crooked Island, Doug and Christel took us to neighboring Long Cay for a day of fishing, snorkeling and beachcombing. Long Cay's north shore is a postcard from paradise. Miles of beach go decades between footprints. One of these days Chris Columbus's wallet will turn up and I want to be the one who finds his driver's license. I'll bet he wasn't even an organ donor.

We found a spot, tossed Rubber Ducky's anchor and immediately noticed two large barrel-like objects stuck in the shallow surf nearby. Wading closer it was clear that's exactly what they were. Wooden barrels. They looked old, really old.

Numerous Spanish galleons sank in the Crooked Island Passage during the 1500 and 1600's. Combine a treacherous barrier reef with unwieldy, often overloaded ships weakened by weather and worms, and disaster was only one storm away. It's not hard to imagine the loot that lies buried beneath the sandy ocean bottom or hidden in coral caves. It's equally not hard to imagine that through some change of current or fluke of underwater nature, it could someday wash up on shore.

I pictured a sailor on an unlucky galleon sailing from Central America after plundering gold, emeralds and whatever else wasn't nailed down. Cue the storm. The hidden reef. Lay in the sickening crack of wood against coral. My sailor, who is actually a nice guy and the only one of the crew to have paid a fair price for his gems, knows he's doomed. The mast cracks, the men scream, the bow lurches high into the sky before the ship's final slide into oblivion. Looking around (desperately) for somewhere to hide his prize, he grabs onto a barrel lashed to the gunnel and pries open the lid...

Snorkeling was shelved, picnic postponed. For the next hour we shoved, pushed and rolled the barrels closer to shore only to have them tumble away on the backside of a wave. Breathless and laughing, I didn't at first notice when Fritz moved off to the side. I looked up when he started to slap the surface of the water and shout.

If you've never seen one, a shark's dorsal fin looks in person exactly like it does on a television or movie screen, only scarier. The physical shape of the word ominous is black and triangular. It comes complete with a soundtrack. You know which one.

I froze.

Fritz said, "No big deal. He's not acting crazy. We'll keep an eye on him."

Doug, furthest away, shouted, "What kind is it?"

"Not sure, but not a nurse."

"We could wait on the beach 'til it swims off," Christel suggested.

Fritz shrugged. "I'll watch him. If he starts swimming erratically we'll move off."

"What does that mean, swimming erratically?" I asked him.

"Means he's hungry."

Christel and I eased over closer to Doug. While Fritz stood guard we finally wrestled one of the barrels onto the beach. Soon after, the not-a-nurse shark (considered harmless) with the full belly took its large teeth and creepy triangle elsewhere. We heaved the other barrel ashore. Doug had a gaff (a metal hook used to bring fish into the boat) and we commenced to hack.

Hardened molasses, while potentially a great preserver of rare gemstones, in this case, was not. I revised my story to star a lazy, unimaginative sailor who, had he ever gotten his hands on gold or gems, would have selfishly clutched them to his bosom as his ship went down and the sea enveloped him. That may sound mean, but we still had to wade back to Rubber Ducky.

I needed something to take my mind off sharks.

Armando and his flying machine

One of the views that started it all...

The mighty mailboat - always a welcome sight

MV San Diego: Motley Queen of the Seas

Not much more than a sandbox

Whole lotta concrete and rock

Finally, a floor

One, two, three...wall!

Underway on San Diego

Waterspout: Tornado at sea (this one got our attention!)

Our oceanside cottage comes to life (view from the south)

View from the north/ocean

Esme: World's best sandog

Connie-Mom braves the channel

Underwater wonderland

The Great Christmas Lobster

Chapter 15
<u>Transitions</u>

In early May we poured the final bond-beam on the front wall, signaling the end of two months of laying rock. We wouldn't miss dancing to the tune of the cement mixer. Thirty feet long, eight feet high with both ends wrapping back another six feet, the wall stood like a monolith in the sand, presiding over the catacombs of the split level structure below. I breathed easier now that we were ready for next winter's building phase.

We prepared *San Diego* for the four hundred mile return to Florida. Winds had settled, towering cumulous clouds remained almost stationary and the sea was a gently undulating carpet of blue. Perfect motorboat weather.

Early one morning, Doug and Christel waved goodbye from the beach as we rowed out and hoisted the dinghy aboard. The Detroit Diesel whined and Bird Rock Lighthouse slowly dipped below the horizon as we motored NW at 8 mph. We put into the south end of Cat Island that evening, with nary a bite on the fishing line.

Toward the end of our second day at sea, we hooked into a ten-pound mahi-mahi. Hand over hand, I brought it alongside, already smelling grilled fish. With a lifting swing I arced the shimmering burst of green and yellow towards the boat. At the top of the arc the fish spit the hook and plunged to safety. The hook, with its chartreuse plastic squid, dropped on deck with a tink.

We were just approaching a reef-strewn entrance through the northern Exumas to the Bahama Banks. It was after eight and the light was fast fading as I steered around a rocky spit into the calm lee of the nearest cay. Mari dropped the anchor in fifteen feet of water with a sand bottom and we shut down for the night.

At two a.m. I was awakened by an uncomfortable roll and went out on deck to see what was up. Foggy from sleep, I couldn't for the life of me figure out where we were. It definitely wasn't where we'd dropped anchor. I made my way forward to check. No anchor. We were on the move.

I woke Mari and turned on the depth sounder. It read forty feet. I quickly got out our second anchor, attached extra line and tossed it over the side. When I was satisfied we were secure, we set about trying to find our location. Based on the red flash of a distant radio tower, the configuration of the nearby cays and the fact that we were on the wrong side of those cays, it slowly became clear.

We'd lost the bitter end of our anchor line where it had been properly cleated off but with not much of a tail. Rocking wave action had eventually tugged the line off the cleat. While we slept, the tide had returned us unscathed through the narrow, rocky channel and into the sound, not far from where we'd caught the fish. If the weather remained calm and we stayed put we'd be okay until morning. I didn't get much sleep.

At dawn we eased our way back to the approximate spot we'd anchored to dive for the missing anchor. I was confident we'd soon spot the hundred-foot line and section of chain, but a half-hour spent zigzagging over a wide area turned up nothing. Then the jellyfish moved in. The spore from the thimble jellyfish is the size of ground pepper and produces a stinging rash beneath elasticized bands of swimming suits. Mari bailed. I stripped and gave it another fifteen minutes without success.

It's a blow to any captain's ego to lose an anchor. I consoled myself with the fact that I never really liked that Bruce anchor. I would, however, miss the line and chain.

As much as we detested Nassau, we needed fuel. By noon we were topped up, chugging past the cruise ships, headed for Chub Cay and a good night's sleep. Flat seas the next day encouraged a non-stop cruise across the Bahama Banks and into the Gulf Stream to West Palm Beach. At some point, for no reason I could figure, our VHF radio stopped working.

At 4 a.m., approaching Florida in a blinding rain-shower, *San Diego* was suddenly caught in a spotlight's bright glare. The U.S. Coast Guard, unable to hail us on the radio, announced through a megaphone they were coming aboard. (Asking permission first would have been nice.) It might have been a training exercise. It took them twenty minutes to launch their inflatable. Once on board, they looked like nervous high school kids shedding water all over the cabin. They called it a safety check and I guess we passed. However, after inspecting our passports they asked for the boat registration and we could not find it anywhere. With the boat rocking, the sky dumping and our cabin filled with dripping boys, the atmosphere began to get tense. Until the young man holding my passport pulled out a folded paper tucked in the cover and said, "Is this it?"

At 8 a.m. we secured the anchor and rowed ashore in search of customs/immigration. Three hours later, we were back on the waterway, headed for Indiantown, a full day's journey in heavy boat traffic. Next afternoon, after transiting the lock into the

Okeechobee waterway, *San Diego* nudged alongside the visitor's jetty at the marina.

Is anyone keeping track of the days? That was number six since leaving Crooked. Add another three before the boat was hauled and tucked into the storage yard. Then we hit the interstate heading for Wisconsin, two thousand miles north.

Picture a scene in rural France during WWII, a bombed-out brick farmhouse surrounded by neglected, overgrown landscape. The interior is a charred ruin, with scorch marks blazed across the walls. Crippled rafters and spongy floors are littered with bits of crumbled plaster. This is what awaited our return from paradise.

He's right. Inside, that's exactly what the house on Washington Island looked like. Outside, the cottage was all charm, even after a fire in 1991, after which I'd indulged a wildly impractical whim and bought the brick shell that remained. A Danish immigrant had built it in 1898 as a wedding gift for his daughter. George Lucke was a farmer who knew how to lay bricks to last. One hundred years and a horrible fire later, the house still stood, but wouldn't much longer without expedient, expensive renovations.

Washington Island is a thirty-minute ferry ride off the tip of the Door County, Wisconsin, Peninsula, the 'thumb' you see on a map that extends into western Lake Michigan. Both my parents were born in rural Door County, near Sturgeon Bay. Though they left the area after marrying, summer trips to the County to visit grandparents, aunts and uncles figured large in my childhood. If Crooked Island was wings, Door County, and Washington Island, was roots.

In recent years Washington Island has evolved from an agricultural to tourism-driven economy. The population swells from six hundred in the winter to several thousand in the summer. New building starts and renovations are almost exclusively for second homes of non-islanders. It's an industry that thrives during the warmer months, a potentially great match for Fritz's skills when our house was far enough along to be considered habitable. He also wanted to set up a shop so he could reconnect with an early and enduring passion: guitar-making.

Our immediate plan was to spend summers bringing the little brick house back to life. The money we'd earned in New Mexico wouldn't last long especially since it appeared, for the next several years at least, that we would be continually under construction. So before our Crooked Island muscles and calluses had a chance to soften, we plunged into months of framing, wiring and plumbing. At least we weren't mixing and pouring concrete.

By mid-October the leaves and the temperatures were dropping. Other than a rusting Franklin stove we salvaged from the Island Exchange, otherwise known as the dump, there was no heat in the house. When the wind blew, it lifted my hair when I stood in the middle of what would someday be the living room. I never thought I'd turn into a snowbird, but sleeping in a down jacket quickly lost its appeal. Even the bats that shared the upstairs loft with us looked cold.

With the ghosts of my Norwegian ancestors murmuring their disapproval, we readied the truck for the move south. Sorry Uncle Ole.

Chapter 16
Terror at Jewfish Cut

You could say our second season officially began when I walked into SaveWay Liquor in Okeechobee, Florida, to buy a bottle of Bacardi Limon for the Indiantown Marina's manager. He had loaned us his turbo-diesel truck to move six-ton *San Diego* from the storage lot to the marina, a task well beyond the range of our Ranger.

With the boat "on the hard," we spent the first day exposed to all sorts of toxicity; Mari scrubbed off six months worth of mold coating *San Diego's* cabin while I slapped fresh antifouling paint on the bottom of her hull. The filthy chores done, we were ready for launch, but only if the travel-lift and its operator were working at the same time.

Once *San Diego* was afloat, we began a five-day shopping spree that laid waste to half our annual budget. It also settled the boat well below her load waterline. The lists of *absolutely need* and *would really like* were pages long, but Home Depot, Sam's Club and Target chewed 'em up and spit 'em out.

On November 10th we fired up the engine, inserted earplugs and headed for the waterway. Stiff easterlies kept us confined to the ditch all the way to Key Biscayne's No Name Harbor. Next morning we walked out on deck in time to see a 60' ketch reach into the harbor with all sails set. Perched on the bow like a figurehead was a topless Valkyrie in bikini bottoms, chest thrust forward, hair streaming behind. It was my fiftieth birthday.

Next was a visit to the small Cuban-run cafe at the head of the harbor. Mari had arranged to have the cook bake me a cake. As he ceremoniously carried it to our table, the wait-staff, the Valkyrie (now wearing a top) and her family joined in for a rousing Happy Birthday. Back on board for a glass of wine at sunset, we spotted a man wearing a suit and tie being rowed out to *San Diego*. I wondered if we'd forgotten to buy a permit or pay a tax. But it was Crooked Island neighbor Woody who had spotted our boat in the harbor. When he climbed aboard and asked if we'd ever had stone crab, I knew my fiftieth couldn't get much better.

With a forecast of SE wind at 5-10 knots and 2-4 ft. seas we left for Nassau the following day, motoring straight through in twenty-four hours. Back at our old roost in the East Bay Marina, I noticed no effort had been made to patch broken portions of the dock. Fuel was no longer available, but they had overnight security.

Taxes and car insurance paid, last minute necessities aboard, we fueled-up the next day and headed southeast. During the night a high-pressure system had settled over the Bahamas resulting in stiff easterly winds. *San Diego* bucked out of the channel with a wicked twist that managed to shake loose a 40'x 40' tarp lashed to the top of the cabin. We chased it but its color matched the ocean and we ultimately lost sight of it in the churned-up seas. I hoped it would wash ashore in New Providence before the plastic packaging disintegrated and the tarp became a hazard to sea life.

For two days we hugged the leeward side of the Exuma chain while the wind blew a steady twenty knots and kicked up a jagged four-foot chop.

We found relief from slamming wind and water only late in the day, after we'd fought our way into some bay or inlet and dropped anchor for the night. Shutting the engine down each afternoon was usually followed by sighs of relief and silence, but for several days, because of the wind, it had little impact on the volume of noise.

It was on one of those evenings when peeling off a swimsuit that my hand brushed against the side of my right breast. And paused. I felt a pea-sized bump through the thin fabric. Fingertips directly on skin, it was harder to detect. Off and on during the night—thanks to the wind, I was awake anyway—I kept returning to it, curious, though not particularly concerned, just yet. I mentally reviewed the risk factors: I was forty-six, which was young, or so I thought, to be a candidate for breast cancer. I was an athlete, not overweight. I'd had a child in my early twenties and nursed for over a year. I didn't drink heavily, had a good diet and as far as I knew had no history of breast, or any other kind of cancer in my family. My last mammogram, eighteen months before, had been clean.

Stress? That was another story. But I'd left all that in New Mexico the previous year. It couldn't count now, could it? While the boat rocked and the wind howled another thought surfaced: When I left my business, I'd dropped my health insurance. While I wasn't completely comfortable with the decision, it was an expensive monthly obligation. I'd been healthy my entire life. I'd sort out some coverage, I thought, when the timing was better.

Next morning I told Fritz what I'd found. It was such a small lump it was hard for him to feel. He asked if I wanted to go back to Nassau for an exam, but the thought of backtracking through what we'd just negotiated seemed worse than living with some uncertainty. I wanted to get to Crooked, get settled. Then we could decide how to proceed.

I thought about how comforting it would have been to pick up the phone and call the Albuquerque doctor who for twenty years had treated my minor complaints. How much I wanted, at that moment, to be sitting in his familiar waiting room. Instead I stood lookout on San Diego's bow, signaling back to the helm a safe route through hidden obstacles.

Like the previous year, we were forced to the south side of Great Exuma but chose a route that would keep us in deeper water about six miles from the coast. We approached Jewfish Cut late in the afternoon, the wind dropping with the setting sun. There was just enough daylight to pick our way through the labyrinth of coral reefs to a protected anchorage in the bight of a small cay. This time, when I shut down the engine the silence was deafening.

I slipped on mask, fins and snorkel and dropped over the side to check the anchor and look for lobster or edible-sized fish. A half-hour later I climbed aboard and suggested pasta for dinner.

A bright half moon lit the sky, muting the stars. The faint glow of Georgetown in the north and the occasional swish or splash around the boat were the only reminders that we weren't alone on the planet. By 8:30 p.m. we were sound asleep.

Shortly after, the roar of an outboard motor jolted us awake. Whoops and hollers, like from a wild party, carried over the engine noise. From the cabin we could see a skiff circling *San Diego*, setting us rocking in their wake. It looked like five men on board.

We watched and waited in the darkened cabin. I hoped they would speed off after buzzing us, but after the third revolution they throttled back and headed toward the boat.

I flipped on the lights and handed Mari the radio.

"I'm going on deck," I told her. "Start calling May Day if it gets ugly."

I stepped onto the engine cover and squatted down as they came alongside. After training in a Tae Kwon Do studio for the last four years I was prepared to deliver a sidekick if necessary. The boat pulled close. They were all seated except the man nearest *San Diego* who stood with his back to me. He wore a long coat and was fumbling with something.

"Calling any station, any station. Come in, please. This is motor vessel *San Diego*, *San Diego*. May Day. Repeat, May Day, May Day, May Day."

I could tell my message was barely intelligible. My lower jaw had started to clatter like the bottom half of a pair of wind-up teeth. I kept repeating the transmission, afraid if I stopped talking, I'd start screaming.

Fritz was arguing with the men in the skiff. They sounded rowdy, possibly drunk. I'd heard stories of people and boats disappearing in the Bahamas, but always thought it was related to the drug trade. Fast boats were commandeered for midnight runs - what could they possibly want with us?

I couldn't think clearly enough to form any plan about what to do if they boarded. I was locked on only one thought: We might not get out of this alive.

I kept my eyes locked on the guy with the coat. As the skiff bumped against *San Diego* he turned around. His hands were empty. Crouched as I was on the engine cover, we were eye to eye. I smelled rum on his breath. I glanced at the others, all bleary-eyed, all Bahamians. No one was smiling.

I kept my tone even and unfriendly. "What do you guys want?"

Coat mumbled, "We wan' mon-."

"What?"

This time he was clearer. "We want money."

"Money," I said. "Are you crazy? You don't come alongside a strange boat at night in the middle of nowhere and ask for money. That is not cool. Don't even think about it! Get the hell out of here! My wife is on the radio right now telling Georgetown what's going on."

The guy sitting at the bow looked up and gave me a cold, sober stare. A few long seconds passed.

Coat made a move to hoist himself over the gunnel.

I readied a kick and said as coldly as I could, "You are not coming aboard this boat."

After a few seconds the guy in the bow nodded at the driver and said, "Let's go."

Coat shoved off and they raced whooping and hollering into the night.

I watched until they were out of sight.

By then the quake in my jaw had migrated to my hands. I couldn't pick up anything without dropping it, but my brain was communicating clearly and I was listening.

No one would come to help us. I knew it. Fritz knew it. Undoubtedly, the men in the skiff knew it. The anchorage was too remote. Even if someone in Georgetown had picked up the transmission, what could they have done?

"We have to get out of here. Now."

"I don't think they'll be back," Fritz said. I knew he was thinking about the coral field surrounding us.

"Maybe they just went to get their friends. They know it's just the two of us. We have to get out of here."

Fritz went on deck and looked around. The sky was clear and the moon gave enough light to spot sandy paths between the reefs. He started the engine.

We hauled up the anchor and with me on the bow, picked our way into deeper water. With the light breeze came quiet seas and by dawn we had reached the south end of Long Island. The weather held and the thirty-mile wide Crooked Island Passage stretched calm and flat in front of us. Without a word we motored on until noon the next day, when we dropped anchor on Crooked's west side, turned off the radio and slept.

Chapter 17
<u>Weathering In</u>

We stood in front of the stone and concrete structure we'd left behind the previous spring and stared. Somehow, we'd forgotten all those sacks of cement, piles of rock and stacks of re-bar. I felt particularly inspired to begin the woodworking portion of the house—I love working with wood and its quirkiness—but our first priority was to get all systems up and running at the Lippincott's so we could move back in.

This is always a major task on Crooked when something has been left unattended for even a few weeks. It may be the corrosive salt air and humidity or the fact that we're in the Bermuda triangle (or both), but things here break at an unprecedented rate. First on the repair list was a small fresh water pump requiring a three-hour rebuild before we had running water.

The third day ashore I finally got to our container. The rusted hinges squealed when I pried open the doors, immediately followed by the scurry of rats fleeing daylight. Except for the pungent stink of rodent and the stack of windows that had finally arrived after our departure the previous spring, all appeared as we'd left it. Then I got to the stack of tongue and groove roofing. Like an abstract painting, a furry scum of yellow and orange mold streaked with crimson covered the stack of pine boards. Sensing impending doom I surveyed all the other lumber, but the damage seemed confined to the roofing. These boards, a hundred and forty-four of them, had been the most exposed to salt water on the barge. Salt retains moisture; they never really dried out.

We stacked the corrupt pile in the sun then scrubbed each board with a bleach solution to kill the mold. Ultimately, they all had to be sanded and in some cases completely resurfaced with an electric hand planer.

We limited the use of treated timber for the external floor joists, not wanting to surround ourselves with poison-impregnated wood. Laying a yellow pine floor earned neighborhood-wide attention. "Termites," some predicted. "Rot out in a year, " or "You've got more guts than me."

Granted, if a piece of untreated wood is left on the sand for more than a week, termites attack with a vengeance. But I'd seen a house at the harbor built in 1876 with its original wood floors still intact. Many of the local Bahamians spoke fondly of growing up in houses with "board" floors. Like the floor in the harbor house, every piece of our untreated wood was at least three feet off the ground.

The season's first visitor arrived and our work crew increased to three. We hugged hello, then handed my sister Carla a wide straw hat and pair of gloves. She was the crowbar person. Very few of the tongue and groove planks fit easily together - Carla's job was to apply necessary leverage to convince a reluctant board to see it our way. Mari fetched planks and held the ends in place while I hammered home the 16-penny galvanized nails. Some boards still resisted our combined efforts but my liberal use of four-letter expletives usually did the job. I saved major explosions for the times I missed the nail and whacked my hand.

Carla went with me the day I went to see the nurse in Landrail. It was Beulah Carroll's job to patch, stitch and medicate the entire island between infrequent visits from a traveling "Crown" doctor. She wasn't sure what to make of the lump I'd found, but the doctor was due to visit the island later that week. When I returned to the clinic to see him, he examined me and pronounced it a cyst. Not to worry, he said, and advised me to have it checked when I returned stateside in the spring.

Call it intuition or sixth sense. I wanted to believe him, but didn't. Or at least I remained suspicious enough to want a second opinion. If it meant flying to Nassau, I would go. In the meantime I had a plateful of diversion. Carla was there, and within weeks Connie, and then Seth would arrive. The wood floor was adding a homey dimension to the rock and concrete fortress we'd created. Then there were the fireworks to look forward to every time Fritz missed the nail-head he was aiming for. I might have been far away from medical care, but I wasn't alone.

My vision of completing the floor before rain interrupted ran afoul of my two female construction partners whose daily agenda included snorkeling, beachcombing and food preparation. Since I was forced to go along with this plan, I generously devoted time to spearfishing and kept seafood on the table.

Even so, a week later we had a completed 30-ft. x 28-ft. floor on which to build the remaining wall sections. Not only was this a great space for framing and painting the walls, it made a perfect party platform. When each section of the wall was complete, we filled a tub with cold beer, then went door to door to invite nearby neighbors for a wall-raising. The only caveat was that the wall had to be up and bolted in place before anyone cracked open a can.

It might have been better to announce it on the VHF. Once word circulated that everyone had fun, some wondered why they hadn't been included. This added an unexpected social spin we'd have to take into account for any future projects requiring a community assist. On a sparsely populated island it pays to avoid conflict and hurt feelings. We just didn't know if we had enough beer.

Making a call with a VHF radio in lieu of a telephone was like learning a whole new language. It was also like declaring open season on privacy.

Once reaching your party on Channel 16, you switched to a working channel to keep 16 open for other people who wanted to make calls, or for emergencies. In our neck of the airwaves working channels were 14 and 12. People were always forgetting to switch from Channel 16, though. You could hear the silent groan in someone's voice the moment they realized they'd been broadcasting their conversation island-wide.

But even if you did remember to switch to a working channel, the island switched, too. In fact, some houses had their radios set to toggle right along whenever a channel was changed. And some, who did more listening than calling, left the dial on 14 more or less permanently. (Slow switchers didn't want to risk missing the least little conversational morsel.)

All sorts of linguistic games, codes and deliberately veiled exchanges had been developed to confuse VHF voyeurs. Often they even confused the person they were intended for.

One morning we were on board *San Diego* in the middle of a messy engine repair when we heard Marina Gibson calling us: "*San Diego*, BASRA One."

I left Fritz up to his elbows in grease and grabbed the receiver. "BASRA One, this is San Diego."

"One-Four please."

"One-Four."

"How you doing?"

"Very well, thank you Marina. How are you doing?"

"Pretty well. Pretty well. You could stop by today."

"Ah, okay. Is there something...? Do you think... Any particular time?

"Yes, yes. You could stop by."

"Okay. Both of us?"

"Have a pleasant day."

"Well, thank you, you too. We'll be standing by 16."

We cleaned up, rowed to shore and drove to Landrail but by then Marina wasn't in the restaurant. We waited, but finally left and returned several hours later. She was in the kitchen kneading bread. She had called, she said, to tell us we were getting a phone call that evening at seven.

Why couldn't she tell us that on the radio? It just wasn't done.

Learning everyone's radio names, or handles, made it easier to read between the frequencies. When Sweet Pepper called Wild Tamarind, Miss Viola's arthritis was acting up. When Sweetwater called Pittstown, Carter had fish for sale. Occasionally, though, emotion trumped protocol. When Pittstown Point's manager

Tammy caught, then released, the heart of a high-strung yachtsman, he openly broadcast his despair before sailing off into bad memory. "Tell Tammy I love her," he wailed into his receiver until the message grew faint, singing his own version of the Channel 16 blues.

After two days of installing windows and doors, we were ready to tackle the roof. The backbone of the gabled design was a laminated ridge-beam that spanned the width of the house. We also installed a support post in the center to aid in wind loads (think hurricanes). We were blessed with a stack of quality yellow pine lumber for the thirty-eight rafters that Mari and I eased, one at a time, into place. Six galvanized spikes held the rafters to the ridge-beam, while the other end was securely fastened to steel hurricane straps we'd embedded in the concrete wall at the front of the house. Steel straps also held the rafter ends that rested on the framed section of wall. If there was ever any doubt about how many nails to use, I imagined a 200 mph blow and hammered in a few more.

By now the exposed ceiling boards had thoroughly dried from the bleach treatment—no further hint of mold—and were ready to lay them in place. My sister had just left so it was Mari and me on the roof for five days of nailing and gluing. A fresh NE wind took the bite out of the sun.

Once the boards were laid, things moved quickly. We rolled out tarpaper, tacked it down, then covered the works with 4-ft. x 8-ft.

sheets of foil-backed foam insulation. We hoped this would cut the heat and mute the sound of rain on the metal roof.

The galvalume steel roof panels still lay in a strapped bundle in the container, untouched since arriving the year before. With the lumber now out of the way I could finally reach the sheets at the back of the container. I cut the straps and began pulling out each 16-ft. x 2-ft. piece. Each one was streaked with corrosive looking white powder. Wondering why a stream of foul language was suddenly emanating from the container, Mari climbed in to have a look.

"Oh my God," she said. "What should we do?"

"Beats me. I have no idea what's going on."

It took two hours to get through to the manufacturer on the phone, but a fraction of that time for them to tell me what was what was wrong. It was white rust. The shipper should have cut the straps on the bundle when it had arrived in Miami. When I asked how the shippers were to supposed to know this, the manufacturer's representative replied, "They just should have known." Before hanging up she added that since it was an export order there was no warranty and therefore entirely my problem.

I was too disgusted to call back for advice about possible remedies. Instead we spent a couple of hours with a scrub brush, which took care of the cosmetics, but the coating had definitely been compromised. We hoped it would last for at least a few years.

There was another surprise at the bottom of the pile. When the bundle had been picked up by the shipper's forklift to be loaded into the container, the four bottom panels were carelessly gouged. Two panels were partially salvageable, two completely lost. By now I was getting sick of Expensive Lesson #4. How many more times would we get slapped?

Another high-pressure system locked the Bahamas in a windy embrace, with twenty-knot gusts from the NE. We staged the 16ft. panels on the west side of the house. Jockeying one panel at a time, Mari climbed up to the step-ladder's second rung, then raised the panel about six inches above the roofline where I grabbed it with gloved hands. From here she hoisted the lower end while climbing the ladder until we could rotate the sheet over the roof edge. Each time, the wind briefly caught the panel and it fluttered like a huge metal flag until I slammed it down flat on the roof. From there I could drag the piece into place as long as I didn't lift the edge more than two inches. Once in position, I quickly secured the panel with four screws and then we'd repeat the whole process. In two days the roof was completely covered. All that remained was driving in an additional eight hundred screws.

Finally, a bug-free space to ourselves. The bananaquits and hummers that had been darting carefree through our window spaces were relegated to the outdoors. We invited the neighborhood to help us celebrate. We could have had a sock hop on the open pine floor, but nobody had socks.

Chapter 18
Topic of Cancer

"If you're going to have cancer," Dr. Cartwright said, "this is the kind you want."

I sat in Marina's phone hut and listened while he negotiated Nassau's traffic on his way to a lunch meeting. When I'd returned his call, his nurse had given me his cell phone number. She apologized and explained that he would have waited for my call in his office, but he was the meeting's guest speaker.

That's when I'd known his news wouldn't be good.

"I shouldn't be telling you this on the phone, " he said. "I should be sitting across from you, holding your hand."

I would have started to cry then, but there were people waiting to use the phone and I didn't want to make a scene. Besides, Dr. Cartwright wasn't finished with me yet.

"What will you do?"

"Um. I'm not sure. Go back to the States, I guess." The woman talking was using my voice but she sounded far away, like on Neptune.

He went on to describe my prognosis in glowing terms. Stage 1! Slow-growing tumor! Probably just a lumpectomy! Just when it started to sound like a frolic with dolphins, the car noise quieted and he delivered his punch line.

"My family and I will pray for you."

Enough! This kind man had just told me I had breast cancer. Did he have to rip out my heart, too?

I waited for Mari in the truck. When she stepped out of the phone shack I saw by her look there was dirty weather ahead. She climbed in without a word and stared straight ahead. We rolled down the road a short way before she dropped her face in her hands. "I have cancer."

I made a pathetic attempt to comfort her, but she pushed away my hands. I think she wanted to be on a mountaintop, screaming.

Even though I was prepared for the news, my brain was in turmoil. Fix-it solutions spun chaotically as I tried to weigh all the factors. I spewed out a few possibilities, but Mari was in no mood to listen. It was a long ride to the house. A couple of days later I could tell she'd found her center again. From there we moved ahead.

So. A month of phone calls, two trips to Nassau and one biopsy later, it appeared we had some new plans to make. And now that I knew my little lump was an unfriendly sort, I was ready to take a filet knife and be done with it. I wanted it OUT.

Complicating matters was the fact that we had, at the moment, no "home." With roots still so recently upended in New Mexico, though, it seemed the best choice to return there for whatever was next. Ironically, I had far too many female acquaintances to ask when searching for a physician referral. I suddenly realized that my expressions of sympathy to women I knew who'd had the disease had been nothing more than lip service. I may have clucked and shaken my head at the tragedy of it all, but I'd never really listened. It hadn't seemed to have anything to do with me. Until, obviously, now.

The surgeon I contacted handled only breast cancer patients and was extremely busy. Good, I guess. Who wants a surgeon who sits around waiting for the phone to ring? Bad, because it made clear the epidemic proportions the disease had attained. I couldn't get an appointment for five weeks.

It helped tremendously that Dr. Richard's nurse was really Zena, Warrior Princess, out of costume. She talked me through the entire process, from getting my Nassau records to chilling out about the wait. Based on my type of tumor a few weeks would not make a difference, she said. (Note to family: If I'm ever on a high, narrow ledge looking down while in a poor frame of mind, call her first.)

As she so often has, Carla rescued me, insisting that I stay at Tinkertown during my recovery, however long it took. (Carla taught Zena all her tricks.) Seth was also in Albuquerque, having just returned from his recent two-week visit to Crooked. He was teaching preschool and deciding how serious he wanted his current relationship to become.

Connie arrived for a five-month long stay on Crooked, a trial run we'd suggested to see if she really wanted to permanently roost. Now that we had walls and a roof, Fritz and I set up a temporary kitchen and moved into our own house, leaving Woody and Shirley's to Connie's care.

I ran every morning, training for surgery like it was a marathon. From the front of our house I jogged east along the beach to the base of Gun Bluff, a hundred-foot rocky outcropping topped with a house, the most remote residence along the north shore. The owners, who lived in Alaska, weren't often there and didn't mind friendly trespassers. Steps cut into rock descended from the bluff into the quarry once used to harvest rock for the lighthouse, now planted with salmon-colored bougainvillea, coconut palms and sapadilly trees. There were more steps to the next stretch of beach, then another, smaller bluff to the third. The last bluff was the hardest to climb but the beach beyond offered hard-packed sand at low tide, suitable for mind-emptying sprints.

Each day I brought back a beach-found talisman: a lightbulb (useful at the end of a tunnel), a buoy (for staying afloat), many shells (still beautiful, though chipped). Fritz and I decided I would return to New Mexico alone for the first appointment with the surgeon. Once I knew what he recommended, we'd take the next step.

In mid-February, 2000, I left Crooked Island and flew to Nassau, by then wishing BahamasAir offered frequent-flyer miles. My flight to the States wasn't until the next day; I grabbed a taxi and asked the driver to make one stop before dropping me at the hotel. Once in my room I locked the door, filled the tub with the hottest water I could stand, climbed in and drank an entire bottle of champagne.

I kept myself busy and waited for news. My mother often dropped by to offer her help, but it was soon clear to both of us that much of the work, like plumbing and electrical, I had to do myself. Connie began teaching a weekly crafts class at the local high school. All of a sudden she had her hands full, juggling thirty-five high schoolers with no fundamental crafts education, like how to spread glue, use materials, draw basic shapes. Their concept of perspective was right up there with Baroque music theory.

Connie's daily visits to our house became bi-weekly. I'd find her hunched over the kitchen table at Woody's immersed in beads, glitter and glue. There was no question she knew how to entertain herself.

Earlier in the season, Connie had asked us to locate a car for her in Nassau. The Daewoo "carlette" as we soon called it, was a cute maroon runabout—Crooked's answer to the Morris Mini. Driving to the village one day I came across the carlette parked beside the road near the harbor. I didn't give it much thought until I found Connie visiting Marina at the Lunchroom.

"What happened?" I asked her. "You run out of gas?"

She shook her head. "No, the engine just quit."

Hmmm, I thought. Rough road - loose wires - battery terminals - maybe something electrical.

Then Connie said, "When I started the car to come here the oil light came on."

"The oil light?" I exclaimed. "You drove the car with the oil light on?"

"I was going to ask you about it."

I have a certain affinity with machines and the thought of that motor running without oil really set me off. Plus, I knew who would have to fix it. "Mom," I said, trying but failing to keep exasperation out of my voice. "You've been driving cars for over fifty years and you don't know better than to shut off the motor if the oil light comes on? There's no telling what kind of damage you've done."

Marina broke in at that point. "You shouldn't talk to your mother like that."

"I didn't drive it very far," Connie protested.

I shook my head, said I'd see how bad it was, and stormed out. Marina wouldn't speak to me for months. My reaction may have stemmed from tension related to Mari's situation, but regardless, I think I'd have been just as angry.

The car's motor had seized, requiring parts ordered from Nassau. The engine had to be completely dismantled, crankshaft polished and bearings replaced. I was not happy about spending two days under that car due to gross negligence. In fact, it was precisely that type of circumstance that had curbed my enthusiasm for my mother's choice to live here. Connie was apologetic and helpful until the incident blew over, but every time I saw that car I shuddered.

It's dark and chilly in the bedroom and I'm drifting in and out of Codeine-induced sleep. I'm minus one pea-sized lump and thirteen lymph nodes. There's a drain under my arm that I'm already itching to pull out. Somewhere in a lab a pathologist is poking around those nodes to see if my lump was the traveling kind. It's day two after the surgery; probably another two before the surgeon calls with news.

Fritz pokes his head in to see if I'm awake. Even in the dark I can tell he's holding something. I sit up in bed as he thrusts his hands forward and deposits a wiggly black ball on my lap. "Carla got you a puppy," he says.

Chapter 19

__Show Goes On__

Anyone I know who has been diagnosed with cancer has gotten very interested, very quickly, about the mind's role in healing. The medical side of treatment is only the beginning.

Somewhere in those early days of trauma and wobbly decision-making ("I still don't believe this is happening, but just in case it is, this is probably what I should do"), questions begin to form. Big questions. Like, where (the hell) did this come from? And, what (the hell) can I do to make it go away and never come back?

There's an exercise in Bernie Siegel's book, *Love, Medicine and Miracles* that asks the reader to identify her "inner guide." Your inner guide is that being who is not you who answers questions like the above that rattle terrifyingly around in your head. The day before surgery I'd been scoffing my way through this inner guide business, asking some pointed and purposefully messy questions, when a new voice weighed in, sounding more than a little annoyed.

She was Deep South with Attitude, like she wasn't about to suffer any fools, especially those of a white, skinny variety. Her name was Esmeralda, same as the life-sized mechanical fortune-teller just inside the entrance to Tinkertown. The museum's Esmeralda accepted quarters in exchange for predicting a small card's worth of someone's future. It was harder to get information out of Esmeralda, my inner guide. Most of the time she'd only snort and say, "It's complicated," though occasionally she'd call me sugar, or baby girl. I loved that part, but there wasn't a whole lot of guiding going on here.

Either the communication problem worked both ways or Esmeralda decided she needed corporeal backup before she'd have a prayer of influencing my stubborn subconscious. Because when the blinds were raised and I looked into my new puppy's old eyes, I recognized some heavy wisdom even before I heard Esmeralda chuckle.

By now you're thinking the Codeine was a wee bit strong, but really, these are the reflections of a sane, though temporarily wounded person. All I can say is, when you ask for help, you get it. It's complicated.

This puppy had been left at the feed store where Carla bought hay for her horses. She and two male siblings were awaiting their fate in a cardboard box after being orphaned when a rancher shot their trespassing mother, who'd probably been looking for food. Carla knew that no matter how successful the surgery, I faced recovery time and possibly further treatment. She also knew how close I'd been to Leon, my German "keep me away from water" shepherd. She picked up the first puppy to wiggle toward her when she knelt close to the box, then told the clerk she might have to bring it right back.

This was a handsome pup, well proportioned and all black except for a white star on her chest. She had piercing amber eyes that locked on to whomever was talking. The closest anyone could come to determining her breed proposed an odd mix: black Lab and pit bull. I named her Esmeralda.

Fritz and Carla found a dog crate and moved it into the bedroom. The next day, I was up and around and able to help with some early puppyhood education. Esme quickly adapted to going outside to relieve herself, even in foot-deep snow. In fact, she loved it: spring, leap, tumble, repeat.

When the phone rang on the Sunday following the surgery I thought it was probably Seth checking in. Instead, after Fritz and the caller exchanged a few words, he handed me the phone to me and said, "It's your doctor."

"Hi," I said. "How are you doing?"

"Fine, thank you. And how are you feeling?"

"Pretty good, I guess. Ready to get rid of this drain."

"Well, we think you're pretty good too," he said, and I could hear the smile. "The margins were completely clean and there is absolutely no lymph node involvement. It's a great result - the best it gets. Congratulations."

There was more, but Esmeralda the inner guide was cheering and Esmeralda the puppy was barking so it was kind of hard to hear.

Our lives made an abrupt U-turn on the phone call from the surgeon. Months of tension spontaneously released from my pores. I was giddy for two days, unable to concentrate. Mari came back to earth before I did, suggesting I return to Crooked to continue work on the house during her six weeks of follow-up radiation. She had a point; my moral support was no longer an immediate need. I flew east.

Connie met my plane. We had a lot to thank her for. Without her support and some frank negotiations with the hospital we might have had to abandon Crooked Island altogether. She'd had her hands full with the high school kids and the carlette was stuffed with boxes of craft supplies. Silver and gold beads and flakes of rainbow glitter were now part of the upholstery.

But now, electrical wiring and plumbing were the new priority. The composting toilet, while great in theory, proved to be far to attractive to the insect population to even consider moving it indoors. Conventional plumbing won out and I found myself faced with further excavations for the septic tank and drain field. Again, I was grateful for sand.

Along with the advent of an island-wide electric grid came electrical inspectors. For some reason, the Bahamian government chose to use the Canadian Electrical Code even though nearly all electrical supplies came from the U.S. and met U.S code. So there I was, painting black wires white and mixing copper and aluminum wiring in the house to grid connections.

The one good thing to come out of it was a clause that allowed the meter to be out on the road. Our house was 300 ft. from the road and BEC (Bahamas Electric Company) wanted three thousand dollars to run a line from the road to our house. Plus, I would have to dig the trench. I dug the trench anyway, but for two hundred dollars installed my own direct burial wire out to the meter.

Before wiring the house, I'd arranged with Clinton Scavella, a local electrician and fishing guide, to oversee my work. The BEC inspector, the dreaded Mr. Green, required a Bahamian electrician to sign off on all electrical work. For a nominal fee, Clinton agreed to this. He'd stop by every few days to make sure I followed the rules. Once he had me re-do all the downstairs wiring that hadn't been run in conduit.

Every week I'd hear another bad-ass Mr. Green story: "*Did you hear what he made so and so do?*" or, "*Those guys will be lucky if they ever get their hook-up okayed.*" Everyone lived in fear; on a whim he could make your life heaven, or hell.

Clinton took a lot of that pressure off. And as it turned out, I had to wait a full year for the final inspection. In the U.S., electrical inspections occur before the walls are covered so the inspectors can see the installation. On Crooked the house had to be entirely finished before inspection. Go figure.

Each day I worked to exhaustion to keep my emotions at bay. Since Mari and I had been together, we hadn't been apart for more than a few days at a time. This long-term separation was the pits. Occasionally, Doug and Christel would haul me off to go fishing or Connie would fix me dinner or show up to help lay rock. These brief interludes helped save me from myself.

In May, I took *San Diego* back to Florida on my own. Had it not been for the autopilot, this would have been nearly impossible. Flat seas allowed for a shorter, deep-water route back. I made two overnight stops, one at Chub Cay and the other at Bimini. Both times I arrived at dusk to surprisingly empty anchorages with earplugs in place and felt immense relief when the motor was shut down. When I removed the earplugs, though, the roar of each island's diesel generator stomped on any semblance of peace and quiet. I slept with earplugs.

I hitched a four-knot booster ride in the Gulf Stream all the way to Stuart and by evening the following day, *San Diego* had been tucked away at Indiantown for the season.

Now I realized what an impact Esme the dog would have on our lives. Instead of a straight shot north to Wisconsin where Mari could easily have flown to meet me, there loomed a major cross-country zigzag in the Ranger.

I was driving all the way to New Mexico from Florida to pick up a puppy that needed a ride to Wisconsin.

Chapter 20
<u>Bilge Pumps, Dog Hair & A Fowl Encounter</u>

San Diego's compact cabin reeked of wet dog. Esme was curled in a tight black ball below the bunk, taking shelter from the incessant thunder. This was our first trip to Crooked with our eight-month-old canine companion. Esme was now thirty pounds of eager love and joy with penetrating amber eyes that could melt or (we hope) freeze hearts. She was our first line of defense against unwanted boarders. I hoped as long as no one knew how friendly and gentle she was, her stocky build and remarkably large teeth would keep uninvited visitors at bay.

While I have never believed carrying weapons aboard was a good idea—during my years sailing it always seemed that boats with weapons found more trouble than they repelled—neither Mari nor I wanted another scene like the previous year at Jewfish Cut.

Hunkered down at Indiantown Marina, we pumped rainwater from *San Diego's* bilge and waited for a weather break. When a clear and quiet Sunday dawned, I fired up the Detroit Diesel and we chugged thirty miles east to the waterway, glad to escape the confines of the marina. It would take another day for the seas to lay down, so we pulled into a popular weekend anchorage just south of Stuart, Florida, for a puppy training session. A half-dozen assorted boats swung at anchor around us but their occupants had all gone to the nearby beach. The tangy scent of surf hung like fog and breaking storm waves vibrated the air.

I'd built a boarding ramp for Esme which both Mari and I had thought a great idea. Now all we had to do was convince Esme to agree. The 1½-ft. wide, 8-ft. long plank clamped onto the gunnel. A line to a cleat controlled the lower end so I could adjust height of the plank in the water. For traction, I'd nailed a thin strip of wood every eight or so inches. What more could a dog want?

Once the ramp was affixed, I dove in, positioned myself at the bottom and called Esme. She leaped forward, then saw what I had in mind. Anxious to please, she ventured a few tentative steps onto the plank, but not even her usual enthusiasm for the water could entice her to descend.

Mari pitched in with cheery variations of "C'mon, girl! You can do it!"

Esme sat at the top of the plank and stared at me.

I crawled onto the lower part of the plank, while explaining how easy it was. Now carrying triple its designed weight capacity, the board was damn shaky. It was all I could do to keep from tumbling off into the water. I crawled up as far as I dared then patted the board in front of me. "It's perfectly safe," I coaxed. "You can do this."

I backed down and she crept after me until she'd made it about halfway. Mari moved in to block any retreat and we ramped up our cheerleading with a string of "Go for its" and "You can do its!"

I backed away from the end of the board, treading water and urging Esme on. I could see she was thinking hard about trying to turn around but finally must finally have thought, "Ah, what the hell." Three more shaky steps and she took the plunge. And instantly a roar of cheers and applause erupted from all the boats in what we'd thought was a deserted anchorage.

For her encore, once I had the plank depth adjusted to her liking, Esme clawed her way back aboard. A few more practice runs, a handful of treats, and you'd have thought she'd been using the ramp all her life. Once underway, this little training session really paid off when we'd pull into an anchorage in late afternoon. Rather than having to launch the dinghy from the cabin roof, we could set up the ramp and say, "Go to the beach," and away she'd swim. Sometimes we'd swim in with her but mostly she was on her own, chasing gulls, husking coconuts or digging holes in the sand.

Next morning, after a fuel stop for the boat and pit stop for Esme, *San Diego* churned out the Jupiter Inlet at dawn into a softly undulating pearl-gray sea. The NOAA weather forecast called for swells of less than two feet so we crossed our fingers and set a course for Nassau, thirty hours down the road.

Twenty-four hours later we rounded the corner of the Berry Islands and Esme had yet to pee. The wind had settled in from the northeast at ten to fifteen knots pushing up a four-foot swell that gave *San Diego* an awkward roll. This combined with Esme's fastidious nature made it impossible for her to take care of business. She had reluctantly relieved herself on the foredeck in the past, something we had counted on for this long passage. Even changing course to run with the swells didn't quiet the ride enough for her to venture a squat. I went so far as to demonstrate how easy it was. But nooo, she insisted on suffering with dignity.

Nassau was still six hours away and since we hadn't officially cleared into The Bahamas I didn't think we should put her ashore. My argument that bladder pressure would eventually force her back to the foredeck didn't sit well with Mari who was near tears and sharing ghost pains with Esme.

When Nassau Harbor hove into view Esme was huddled under the bunk trembling. If we'd had a cell phone, Mari would have already reported me to the SPCA. Inside the breakwater *San Diego* once again became a solid, flat platform. A giant Disney cruise ship towered to port, disgorging color-clad passengers for their six hours ashore. Many lined the upper deck rails watching *San Diego* pass by.

Esme chose this moment to squat at the bow and let loose her golden stream. A full minute later she hadn't moved and a yellow river ran thirty-five feet down each side of the boat ending with a prodigious cascade off the stern and into the harbor.

Greatly relieved, we settled in at our old haunt, the East Bay Marina, which hadn't fared well with Hurricane Hugo. The fractured hulls of several boats lay sunk at their moorings. The sound of hammers and pry bars competed with conch vendors under the bridge to Paradise Island. What once was grim was now ugly and all of Nassau was busy patching things up.

We tied *San Diego* onto what remained of the outside jetty next to the now defunct shower stall. Esme was snoozing in the sun on the foredeck when a linebacker-sized Bahamian man carrying a mini-fridge came barreling around the corner of the shower stall. I looked up from where I'd been cleaning dog hair from the bilge pump in time to see Esme leap up with a growling bark I'd never heard, completely transformed into a Tasmanian Devil. Teeth, hair and eyes were all business. The guy with the fridge spun 180-degrees and vanished before she could follow threat with action. A few reassuring words later her hackles went down, her tail wagged and she presented her butt for a rub.

Did our sweet puppy with the amber eyes and bladder of steel have our welfare at heart? Unquestionably.

November 19th

Hi Mom-

Hard to believe we left the States less than a month ago. It only took us a week to get from Florida to Crooked, even with a day and a half in crazy Nassau. Esme was a champ on the boat, though someday I'll tell you about the passage from Florida to Nassau. Next time: different route.

It took us awhile to get the boat unloaded when we reached Crooked—it was too rough at the village jetty to tie up there for several days. Hurricane Somebody or other crumbled half the structure a few years back and no one has bothered to repair it. I'll admit not knowing whether or not the dock will hold the weight of the truck adds to the excitement of unloading. As a bonus, there's now a very nice vinyl-cushioned bench a little ways off in the rocks. It makes a fine place to sit and watch all the daily activity, which mostly, is none.

I had a wonderful surprise waiting for me when we got to the house. Last spring, while I was glowing (radiation) in New Mexico, I knew that Fritz and Connie had finished the stone walls and steps leading up to the west entrance of the house. What he didn't tell me was that he'd taken every lucky talisman I'd picked up on my beach runs last winter and placed them into the walls. The light bulb, the buoys, the shells and even the goofy plastic bits I can't even remember why I picked up. Center stage is our empty New Year's Eve champagne bottle.

Every time I walk up or down the steps I'm reminded how grateful I am to have moved beyond that experience. I know I've said it before, but your love and support meant the world to me, as always. It was an auspicious start to our third Crooked Island season, until the one thing I worried about with bringing a puppy here almost came to pass a few days ago. Remember me telling you about our closest neighbors, Don and June McMillan? They have three grown children and several grandchildren in Toronto, but here on Crooked the closest thing they've got to a relative is an eleven-year old chicken named Henrietta.

Henrietta sleeps in a specially designed cage at night but roams the grounds of their wonderfully haphazard estate, Capistrano, during the day. Breakfast is at eight, afternoon cheese at four. Lately Henrietta has been hiding during the day and this upsets Don no end. "Jeeze," he says, "you'd hardly know we *had* a chicken." But when June calls, Henrietta never fails to answer with what sounds like a cross between a coo and a gurgle. They're a very close-knit threesome.

Last Saturday, Esme and I walked over to visit Don and June. One thing led to another and pretty soon we were all back by the garden checking out the bougainvillea in bloom and the baby tomato plants June had set aside for me. I completely forgot about Esme until she suddenly bolted off barking madly into the bush. Shortly after there was a loud squawk followed by the sound of wings flapping while tumbling in leaves. Then, except for June screaming "Henrietta!" and me screaming "Esme!" there was nothing for a full, horrible minute. I mean it. Dead silence. No trace of dog or chicken.

Could I live on Crooked Island knowing it was my dog that dispatched Henrietta?

Esme finally showed. No feathers in her teeth, at least. I marched her home, then came back to help search and heard June calling from deep in the bush. "Hen-ri-et-ta, please answer me. You can have any kind of cheese you want."

We looked for that bird, or at least her remnants, until Fritz and I had to go to the airport to pick up his mother. June was gracious in her despair but her eyes said killer whenever she looked at me.

The friends we rode with to the airport were not helpful. There were many unnecessarily cruel comments along the lines of finding some barbecue sauce for wings. Getting desperate, I made everyone in the station wagon hold hands while I repeated a lost-chicken mantra. If Henrietta was found whole, hale and hearty, I promised I'd go to services at the Seventh Day Adventist Church in Landrail next week. I knew you'd like that part.

We collected Connie and drove back. I stopped at Don and June's to see if a miracle had occurred, but they were napping, no doubt exhausted by the morning's trauma. The cage was still empty. Fritz's mom and I walked back down at 3:30, the time of day that Henrietta usually hops into her cage, probably anticipating the hors d' oeuvres de fromage on the way. After visiting with Connie for a while, Don disappeared to trim some coconut palms. We had iced tea. I kept my eyes on the door to the cage, which sits about twenty-five yards from the house, and wondered how long it would take to get used to cold winters again.

At 4 p.m., I couldn't stand it anymore. I went outside and walked slowly across the yard. I hope the minister of Landrail's church never finds out what I promised on the way to that cage.

Let's just say he'd expect to see me on a pretty regular basis, topping up the collection plate. If I'd known that darn chicken would be sitting in her cage, looking for all the world like she'd been out for a perm and pedicure, I'd never have gone so overboard. Though I will admit that seeing Henrietta perched there was as close to a religious experience as I may ever have, not counting Camp Lutherdale, summer '69.

I yelled for June and she came running like she was seventeen instead of seventy. We hugged. She yelled for Don. He came. They hugged. June gave Henrietta a fierce, loving look and said, "You must answer me when I call you, Henrietta." Then she went in the house to get some cheese.

Epilogue: My punishment is far from over. At a dinner a few nights ago, Gerry Smith wore a t-shirt with a dead chicken on the front—who keeps these things in their wardrobe?—and I heard clucks throughout the evening. This is a tough crowd, but I don't care. Henrietta is alive and well, Esme wears a leash when visiting the neighbors, and I can sleep at night. Was it luck, prayers or the chicken chant? Just to be safe, on Saturday morning I'll be in the front pew smiling and dropping my thanks in the collection plate. You can't be too careful.

Hope all is well and you don't have too much snow. Miss you!

Love, Mari

Chapter 21

Comfort Zones

Our home was still a skeleton, privacy non-existent unless you call huddling inside the fiberglass shower stall private. The kitchen was bare bones, but the stove was in. My dad, Fred, and his wife Barb arrived for their first visit. Mari hung tarps over the framed wall between the bathroom and our bedroom, though we were still using the composting toilet in the garage. The downstairs guest room was not yet ready for habitation so Fred and Barb shared our open space.

One hot, shirtless night Fred braved a visit to the garage (the rest of us used a bucket after sunset). When he came back he reported, "Didn't see or hear a single 'squito."

Thirty seconds later he started hopping up and down with a piercing yeeeow! His back was covered with those tiny bloodsuckers. I wiped them off but couldn't help with his tormented itching. We put indoor plumbing on the fast track and in two days applauded the first flush.

My dad once built an airplane from scratch. I remembered how the spruce wing components had been meticulously crafted, so I suggested he and Barb make Bahama-style shutters for the garage and guest room from the leftover tongue and groove roofing. They were of simple design: hinged at the top and propped open at the bottom for ventilation and light. Used in conjunction with screens, they were as effective as the jalousie windows we'd installed in the rest of the house.

Mari and I began hanging drywall in earnest. Depending on the humidity, the sheets came out of the container like either wet or dry pasta. It was soon evident that we didn't have enough to finish the job. I couldn't figure out why we had come up short until I realized I'd calculated for the exterior walls, which required only one layer. Not so the interior walls which, of course, take two. (The "ah ha!" moment.) Mari chased down a dozen reasonably price sheets in Nassau and we had them sent on the mailboat. By the time they arrived Fred and Barb were long gone, but they'd left four handsome coral pink shutters.

Mildew is prolific this far south. Consequently, the walls in the house don't extend to the ceiling and, for added ventilation, we chose louvered bi-fold doors throughout. I originally installed a solar siphon for hot water, basically a black coil of copper tubing covered in clear Plexiglas that ran through the water heater for storage. For some unexplained reason, the siphon would collapse every day or two. I finally broke down and hooked up the water heater to electricity, then monitored the electric bill to assess the impact. Our bill went down two dollars. For those hot, windless days when sweat pooled at our feet, the ceiling fans on "high" made a comforting hum and put the cool back in the breeze.

The northeast prevailing winds are cooled by the Atlantic Ocean before caressing the north end of the island. Preceding the cold fronts that have pushed their way down that far, the wind shifted to the south, reminding anyone with a boat on the west side it was time to move. Next, the wind clocked west, then northwest, sometimes accompanied by rain and thunderstorms. Cold fronts were, for the most part, a restorative flush of clean, brisk air that sent any lingering sand flies or mosquitoes tumbling southeast.

Cold fronts were Esme's best friends. The lower the temps the faster the tail-wag. She sprinted for miles on the beach, instilling fear into anything winged. When I tossed a coconut into the heavy surf she'd meet the waves chest first at a full run. I dubbed her the "wave-buster."

Connie arrived and the carlette was soon making inroads all over the island as she planned her next event, a puppet show. How do you say no to a mom who has embarked on a community project and requests your help? Simple answer: you don't. I was delegated the relatively easy task of building the puppet stage. Mainly, this required tracking down a wooden box that had held some telecommunications equipment for the phone company, Batelco. An ideal size, 6-ft. high, 4-ft. wide, 2-ft. deep—all it needed was colorful gingerbread trim and a curtain. A few hours with a jigsaw, sandpaper and spray-paint completed the stage. Another hour or two with the sewing machine and ta-daa: SHOWTIME. (Easy for me to say, I didn't have Mari's job.)

Say hello to Boukee and Rabby, the folk-tale characters who dominate the rich Bahamian tradition of talkin' ol' story. B' Rabby (Brer Rabbit in African-American communities) is a silver-tongued trickster who lives by his wits and loves to outsmart his buddy. It's not difficult. Low-watt B' Boukee is the perfect foil. His greediness lands him headfirst into pots of trouble that Rabby gleefully seasons.

Spend any time in the Bahamas and you'll meet Rabbys and Boukees in every community. Boukee represents all that Bahamians find distasteful: foolishness, greed, dishonesty. Charming Rabby is the archetypal hero-trickster: quick and cunning, an expert at cleverly turning the tables to his advantage and perfectly happy to write his own rules.

Connie borrowed a collection of Rabby and Boukee tales from one of the high school teachers. She picked three and asked if I'd rework them into puppet show scripts. With the craft-class kids making puppets, Fritz on set detail and me at the computer, her production gained momentum. Sort of.

I read through the stories and couldn't imagine these modern-day kids reciting lines, even using puppets, like, "He tell me say you is his father's cart horse and he does ride you everyday." Or, "Oh, we nor bin treat yer good the other day you come." After hours of self-righteous transposing and deciphering I gave Connie some drafts to take to the kids. Ever so proper, I cleaned up ain'ts and make eggs from aigs. And made Rabby and Boukee sound like English gentry discussing high tea.

After the giggling high-schoolers soundly rejected the scripts, I went back to the computer. With Rabby looking over my shoulder, "The Spirit House" turned back into "The Sperrit House" and we were rolling again. I'd now spent so much time with the stories I felt a vested interest in how the show was taking shape and went with Connie to rehearsals. I passed a script to each of the seven students while she admonished, "Take these home and memorize your part! Don't forget to bring them to school with you every day!"

Miss Connie had her hands full. Not only was she the director, she was also the production and equipment manager, as well as the puppet wrangler. And things were not going so well in the corral. The same determination and energy that fueled my mother-in-law's generous nature also nudged her a teeny bit towards favoring the driver's, not the passenger's seat. She had a vision for what those puppets should look like and no amount of cajoling—"That eye is where the nose should be!"—got results.

We rehearsed every day after school. Every day half the kids forgot their scripts and every day another puppet went home with Connie for an extreme makeover. As the big night grew closer, the school decided to add some other songs and skits and turn the whole evening into a fundraiser, saving the puppet show for last.

The show was scheduled to begin at 7pm, which in the Bahamas means you should plan to leave the house by 7:30 unless you live more than twenty minutes away. Once underway, the program maintained a consistent, though not brisk, pace. Hymns were sung, poems recited. After each talent, Assistant Principal Knowles sent ushers through the throng to collect money, then announced the donors, auctioneer-style. If you liked the act, you raised your hand and waved a bill, while Mrs. Knowles shouted, "One dollar from Mari Anderson! Cheer for her!" and the usher snatched it out of your hand. If you didn't like the act, you did the exactly the same thing.

About 9 p.m. Miss Connie stood in front of the group and told us how hard the kids had worked on the production we were about to see. She hoped we enjoyed it. The curtain parted. The tiniest kids had been allowed to come forward and sit in front of the stage. Even from where we sat, we heard them gasp as B' Rabby and B' Boukee marched onstage, ready to rumble.

Chapter 22
The Rescue

Early one January morning, while Mari rode her bike south and I contemplated another day of hanging sheetrock, somewhere in the Crooked Island Passage a boat began to sink.

Doug picked up the faint MAYDAY. As soon as he responded to the caller to verify coordinates, everyone jumped to their VHF radios and cranked back the squelch to listen. I barely heard the numbers through the hiss of the tinny speaker, jotted them down, then plotted the position on a nautical chart. The numbers placed the caller about one mile north of Bird Rock Lighthouse, easily visible from our house.

I trained binoculars on the general area and spotted a sailboat mast. This must be the guy, but this close his radio signal should have been strong unless the set was damaged.

I called Doug to double check coordinates and told him about the mast. The numbers matched but Doug was sure the guy had said he was in a 65-foot sport-fishing boat that was sinking by the stern.

Doug called the MAYDAY to confirm his position. It took a few tries but he finally got an answer. It was a broken, now desperate-sounding transmission: "Ten knots...towar rock...almost... engine. Posi 74-11 west 23...nor..."

"Repeat your position," Doug said.

"74-11 we... 3-09 north."

These were new numbers, plotting out twenty miles northeast of the lighthouse.

Gibson's Lunchroom in Landrail Point was also headquarters for BASRA (Bahamas Air Sea Rescue Association). Marina Gibson called the U.S. Coast Guard—they maintain a substation 150 miles south on Great Inagua—but couldn't confirm a response.

The gas station on Crooked Island doesn't always have gas and this was one of those times. Except for private stashes kept in jugs for emergencies, there was no fuel to be had. Doug didn't have much in *Fishing Machine* so he sent out a call for any boat owner who had gas in the tank. Diesel-powered *San Diego* had plenty of fuel, but her response time would be close to three hours. If we had any hope of reaching the MAYDAY in time, we'd need a light, fast runabout with a big outboard.

Winter residents Lou Soroe and Gerry Smith headed for the airstrip to pre-flight Lou's plane. The winds had been blowing fifteen to twenty knots for days. With the seas running six to eight feet with chop, an eye in the sky was a must. Robbie Gibson, a swashbuckling fishing and SCUBA guide, turned up a barrel of fuel in his garage. He and his brother Don headed for the harbor to fuel up *Thunderbird*, Robbie's 28-foot dive boat powered by a 200-horse outboard.

We didn't know how many people were on the sinking boat or if there were injuries. I figured they could use someone with paramedic training and bailing experience, so I asked Robbie to pick me up off the beach near the airstrip. Doug would stand by the radio and pass on any updates. I arrived just as Lou started his airplane and *Thunderbird* nosed up to the beach. I hopped over the bow and we were off, drywall be hanged.

The nice thing about local knowledge in reef-strewn areas is knowing where the shortcuts are, and we were in a hurry. Robbie had spent almost all his forty years plying the waters around Crooked, but I shot him a glance as we raced toward a huge wall of breakers just east of the lighthouse.

His interpretive powers were acute. "We make it, mon. Don't worry."

Over the roar of the outboard, I heard a low rumble of laughter from Don.

Just when it looked like we'd crash into the reef, the waves parted. I think we were airborne for about five seconds. We slammed back to the water and I asked Robbie if he knew where to go. He opened a locker and a portable GPS tumbled out. He told me to enter MAYDAY's position—it would lead us right to him.

And it would have, had the batteries shown the slightest spark of life. Robbie didn't have any spares so I shrugged and handed it back. I knew we'd get close if we held a heading of twenty degrees, then Lou could guide us in with the plane. Then Robbie reported the compass was screwed up. A quick look confirmed it was out about fifty degrees east.

"Keep the sun on your right and the waves off the starboard quarter," I said. "And let's hope Lou spots 'em."

Doug came on the radio to report MAYDAY's engines had quit and he was going down fast. I had hoped we might get there in time to save the boat, but we were still thirty minutes out. The water in the Crooked Island Passage is two miles deep, but at least it's warm.

Lou shot past us about a hundred feet off the deck. Gerry, using a hand-held VHF, told us to follow them. "No good," I called back and told him about the compass. He said they'd fly back after they found the boat and give us a heading.

We'd been running at twenty-five knots and spending a lot of time airborne. Everything aboard seemed to shake loose and we were soaked. I had to stay crouched behind the center console to hear the radio and couldn't anticipate the boat's gyrations. Robbie cut back to twenty knots so we could keep our teeth.

Ten minutes later, Thunderbird's engine sputtered twice and quit. We looked at each other, then the motor. With all the banging around, there was no telling what had gone wrong. We started madly hunting for loose hoses or leaks. Don discovered a dive tank had shifted just enough to pinch the fuel line. He muscled it off, Robbie restarted the engine and we were on our way again.

While we'd been wallowing I realized just how massive the swells were in the passage. What were the folks in the sinking boat experiencing? We hadn't seen Lou and Gerry for twenty minutes and I began to wonder if they'd spot us, a mere speck, in such big seas. We were over ten miles from Crooked Island. The lighthouse had long since disappeared and we could no longer raise Doug on the radio. We had expected to see the plane by now. Without them, there was little chance of finding that other mere speck.

We passed another tense five minutes, then Robbie spotted the plane far to the west. I called on the radio and a minute later they swept overhead. Gerry told us the boat had sunk just as they'd arrived; there were two men bobbing around in a dinghy. They flew towards the wreckage so we could get an accurate compass bearing. In less than ten minutes we spotted the castaways. Had we kept to our original course, we'd have missed them by two miles.

Lou made a final pass and wagged his wings goodbye. We picked our way through a slick of nautical flotsam to where the men, in a ten-foot inflatable with small outboard, putted in circles. We pulled alongside and helped them aboard, then attached a long towline to the dinghy for the ride back. I noticed there was less than a gallon of gas in their fuel tank. We salvaged a cushion and a few pieces of teak furniture from the wreck but that was all we could save.

The two guys—call them Frank and Tom—were strangely silent. Neither was hurt, so I assumed it was shock. We'd barely begun the return trip when the familiar whup! whup! whup! of the orange Coast Guard helicopter sounded overhead, responding to BASRA's call. We spent ten minutes passing information, including names of boat and owner, over the radio. Frank, the owner, was still dazed. He extracted his passport from a waterproof satchel and handed it to me so he wouldn't have to talk. Tom, the crew, answered the questions himself. Once satisfied, the Coast Guard wished us a safe trip back and we thanked them for their prompt response.

If Frank and Tom were pleased about the Coast Guard presence, they didn't show it.

Robbie cut our speed back to a comfortable twelve knots and tailed after the receding helicopter. I asked him if he was following the chopper and he said yes. I told him I didn't think they were headed for Crooked and gave him a reciprocal compass course to steer. While the compass was wacky, it was at least consistently wacky and the wind and swell direction confirmed my heading.

"You sure?" he challenged.

"I guarantee you in one hour we'll see the lighthouse over the bow." (I figured if I was too far off, the Coast Guard would eventually come back to look for us.)

During the two-hour ride back, Tom kept to himself, but Frank eventually told their story. He'd sold his tech business, bought the boat for a bargain in Nassau and had spent the last two months fixing her up, including extensive engine work. This was the start of a two-year cruise through the Caribbean. Frank had even booked tickets for his kids to fly down and meet him at various islands along the way. Tom, a self-proclaimed "free spirit," had met Frank the previous week in Nassau and signed on as crew.

They'd been en route to the Turks and Caicos. Just past dawn, while Tom was on watch and Frank slept, the high water and high temperature alarms screamed in unison. One of the engines was indeed running hot, a problem Tom had noticed but neglected to report. Responding to the alarms they found the engine room knee deep in water. The bilge pump couldn't keep up.

Why they didn't immediately check hoses and thru-hull fittings can, I suppose, be written off to inexperience and the shock of all that water sloshing around. The fact that lots of engine work had been done in Nassau was a prime indicator that a hose or fitting had come loose. But the answer to that went down with the boat.

Frank had managed to collect most of his valuables before abandoning hope and escaping to the dinghy. Apparently, Tom hadn't been much help when preparing to abandon ship, which explained the absence of camaraderie.

About the time the lighthouse rose above the horizon (whew) Frank remembered his insurance company had insisted he insure the vessel for its full value, exactly double what he paid for it. So it appeared he stood to gain about a quarter of a million dollars from what wasn't anymore looking like much of a tragedy. As that revelation sank in, Frank's mood went from somber to positively chipper.

We pulled into the fishing harbor about noon. The crowd on the jetty wanted details. It didn't take long for a multitude of subtle variations to spawn; soon it was anyone's guess as to what really had happened out there. What I did know is that we were all hungry and Frank needed a drink. That meant Pittstown, where to celebrate his survival Frank set up an open tab for all comers. Free lunch, drinks and dinner made Frank a popular guy.

At one point in the festivities, though, he appeared preoccupied and I asked if he was okay. He nodded, but said his insurance company wasn't sure he'd been covered in Bahamian waters. His lawyer was looking into it and he hoped to know something soon. I'd have been preoccupied, too. Not long after sunset, the news came and Frank's spirits once again soared. He chartered a flight out the next day.

Tom, apparently not sure what to do with himself, hung around Landrail Point for a while. Occasionally we'd see him ambling through the village. After a few weeks he too disappeared. For his efforts, Robbie was awarded the dinghy and outboard we'd towed back.   And I got a free lunch and a day off from hanging drywall.

Chapter 23
<u>Field Trip</u>

A roof over our heads gave us the luxury of more time in the water and more freedom to explore not only Crooked, but nearby cays. I was particularly keen to visit the Plana Cays, thirty miles east of us. The year before, a professor from the States researching Columbus's first landfall had headquartered on Crooked while field-testing his theories for a proposed new location: Plana. San Salvador had for years worn the official first landfall crown, but this was hotly contested by a small, passionate group of academics.

Even though I had some passionate opinions of my own about Christopher Columbus that had nothing to do with where he first dropped anchor, the idea of this historical treasure hunt was intriguing. I'd started writing a novel with characters and ideas sparked by my exotic surroundings. Just like the professor, I wanted to compare what I imagined to the real thing.

San Diego was by no means a tony pleasure yacht, but she was reliable and safe. So in early March when, theoretically at least, the northeast trade winds had settled, we piled ten people plus camping gear and Esme aboard, and ventured east. At our cruising speed of seven knots, the trip would take about six hours. Naturally the wind picked up once we cleared the barrier reef and entered deep ocean. *San Diego* commenced to roll. Those inclined to queasiness got queasy. A visiting friend of our neighbor Bruce's had the worst case and commandeered the cabin and Porta-potty while the rest of us stuck it out on deck and stopped drinking water.

Nobody brought much food; we counted on catching some fish for dinner along the way. But hours at perfect trolling speed with several lines in the water failed to produce a bite. Then suddenly a line zinged, signaling a fish was on. Whatever it was took off strong and fast. For ten minutes we all took turns reeling, coaxing it closer until we could see what it was. Finally with an arcing leap, a forty-pound sailfish splashed next to the boat, vaulted back up and skewered the tip of its long bill into the hull. It looked like a gleaming dart in a yellow bull's-eye.

We'd never caught a billfish before. Fritz reached over, pried the lure from its mouth and released the fish, assuming it was more sport-catch than entrée. It quickly dropped to the water and disappeared leaving just the tip of its bill in *San Diego's* side. Bruce, who had helped reel it in, watched it swim away. "What a shame," he said. "They are such good eating."

In another hour the westernmost of the two cays materialized as a shimmering dark spot on the horizon. It seemed it was almost always at this point—the beginning of a long approach to a new, unknown destination—that the thrill of the life we'd chosen would lift me above the deck for a bird's eye view of boat, friends, ocean, adventure. Despite the risks, or perhaps partially because of the risks, this felt raw, real and exhilarating.

Late that afternoon, we dropped anchor and began ferrying people and supplies to shore. Fritz found some coral heads and dove for dinner. Eight lobsters later, we'd forgiven Bruce for the sailfish. On shore, folks set up tents then walked the beach as the sun began to set, hoping to see a green flash. Esme retrieved the coconuts we tossed in the water for her.

I looked south and imagined three Spanish caravels under full sail rounding the tip of the island in the dying light.

Chapter 24
<u>Messing About With Boats</u>

It was 7 a.m. on a blustery February morning; wispy clouds sailed in from the north. Esme and I clambered down the stairway for a walk on the beach at low tide. The sight that greeted me was not a pleasant one. A hundred yards down the beach was a forlorn-looking thirty-six feet of streamlined fiberglass, high and dry on the rocks. Like broken wings, the struts of the flying bridge and ungainly outriggers titled at awkward angles.

Thunderbird belonged jointly to fishing guides Robbie and Carter who dreamed of turning Crooked Island into a serious deep-sea sportfishing destination. (Robbie's smaller boat was also named *Thunderbird*.) I ran back up the steps, a dull ache in the pit of my stomach at the thought of delivering this news.

I repeatedly called Sweetwater, Carter's VHF handle, until his deep broadcaster's voice answered. I gave him the grim details. After a long silence, he said, "I'm on my way."

The previous day, with a cold front expected to blow through that night, Robbie had moved *Thunderbird* from her mooring on the exposed west side to the north shore's Portland Harbor. Even though the barrier reef broke the Atlantic's big swell, the waves in the lagoon that night still reached four feet. Thunderbird's anchor had dragged until the nylon rope chafed, then was finally severed against a sharp coral outcropping.

It wasn't long before the whole community appeared at the wreck site. We set two anchors and winched the lines tight, hoping that as the tide rose, we might pull her off the rocks. But with twin props weighted down by two in-board CAT diesel engines, the hull was so deeply buried in the sand it was as if *Thunderbird* had been permanently nailed to the beach.

Carter finally called in the *Victoria*, a salvage vessel whose competent crew extricated the boat without further damage. Six months later, after extensive repairs in Florida, *Thunderbird* was back.

One major reason Crooked has so far escaped big development is the lack of a safe, quiet and accessible anchorage. Our Bahamian neighbors have watched the social structure on nearby islands disintegrate when high rollers come to town. For the most part, they much prefer the idea of modest growth. That being the case, those boats that can't be hauled with a trailer are left to fate and a damn good mooring.

At 33-feet, weighing six tons, *San Diego* is in that category. First thing each morning, I look through the palm fronds out front for the flash of yellow hull. Once satisfied that our luck has held, I can relax for the moment. When the bigger winds blow, *San Diego* ducks, dives, twists and turns on her mooring. And no matter how careful I've been I think about lines chafing with all that activity. My biggest fear is seeing her on shore, like *Thunderbird*. Like everything else we have on Crooked, our boat is self-insured.

When I looked out one morning the boat seemed different, but it was almost an hour later before I realized the mast was gone. I swam out and found it on the ocean floor in a tangle of rigging that had ripped loose from the hull mounts. A fractured section of the hinged aluminum base dangled from a twisted bolt. Without the

mast—a 30 ft. converted utility pole that carried a steadying sail—
San Diego had a corkscrew roll like a barroom bull ride. I used the
dinghy to drag the mast ashore for repairs.

Years before, Don McMillan had salvaged parts from a wrecked
sailboat. He still had the cast base from the deck-mounted mast.
With a big hammer and radical modification to *San Diego's* mast,
I used it to fashion a new and improved mount.

Precaution #1: When *San Diego* is at the mooring for a long
stint, lower the mast.

About three days after a severe storm hits the north Atlantic, a
monster ground swell shows up and breaks heavily on Crooked's
outer reef. A low rumble, like the bass boost from a low-rider,
vibrates the air. At high tide the waves carry over the reef and four
to-five-foot swells surge to shore. San Diego rolls gunnel to gunnel
and her bow pitches to thirty degrees. The dinghy is stashed high
on the bluff's rocks, but I still secure it with lines to the palm trees
or the breaking waves will drag it out to sea.

It was shortly after one of these nerve-wracking episodes that
we'd planned an excursion to Long Cay. With neighbors and picnic
supplies aboard, I turned the key. The engine fired once, followed
by a hard, clanking thunk, then froze. I'd been around engines
long enough to know what that sound meant. There would be no
picnic.

Doug and I dismantled the motor. The 453 Detroit Diesel
weighed five hundred pounds. (Thank you, Doug.) We removed
the cylinder head and jacked the motor two feet up out of the bed,
a delicate process in a rolling boat. We used stout chunks of wood
to wedge the beast in place, but I was still nervous about lying
underneath that hunk of iron. Once the oil pan was off, there was
no mistaking the damage.

Despite the extremely high airlock in the exhaust system the radical gyrations of the previous few days allowed water to make its way into one of the engine cylinders. When the engine fired it slammed the piston into the water, bent the rod and fractured the cylinder liner. We could only hope the crankshaft wasn't bent.

We drilled and tapped the piston head to install a heavy bolt. Then Doug leaned into a four-foot pry bar tucked under the bolt, I wailed away with a three-pound sledgehammer from below, and the bent rod finally popped out. All this without getting seasick.

Some neighbors were flying to Florida for the Miami boat show the next day. I sent along a shopping list and four days later had a complete cylinder repair kit. Mari and I spent a messy, grease-filled day reassembling the engine and bolting it back in place. We reconnected loose wires and fuel lines, crossed our fingers and I turned the key. Hallelujah!

Precaution #2: Keep a softball jammed in *San Diego's* exhaust pipe to keep water out.

When big swells roll in, the locals call it a "rage." We were still at Woody and Shirley's and Mari's son Seth was visiting when a rage moved in late one night. At 4 a.m. he pounded on our bedroom door, shouting, "The dinghy's gone!"

It was chaos on the beach. Doug and Christel's boat, *Fishing Machine*, had broken loose from its mooring and wallowed on the sand. Doug was in the water trying to find the broken mooring line. Waves broke heavily on shore. We managed to help Christel shove the boat back into deep water where Doug secured it with a new line. Even though I'd pulled our dinghy over the high berm in front of the house it was indeed nowhere to be seen.

At first light I ran down the beach, hoping the dinghy had washed ashore somewhere, but no luck. I walked back, kicking myself for not tying the damn thing to a bush. The dinghy itself had positive foam floatation but with the outboard attached, I wasn't so sure. I stood on the highest part of the berm and scanned the turbulence in the lagoon.

About to give up I caught a white flash in a wave, like the belly of a large, dead fish, about a hundred-yards out and a quarter-mile down the beach. I stared, but saw nothing more. Mentally marking the spot, I dashed in for snorkel gear and sprinted down the beach. The sun wasn't quite up; visibility was poor. I swam to the spot, stopping every few strokes to get my bearings. Just as I reached the search zone, I scanned the bottom and there, eight-feet down was the dinghy, the outboard askew on its mount.

Seth and I spent a day dismantling and flushing the outboard, which now sported an official-looking Crooked Island patina. After the appropriate amount of cussing, I pulled the starter cord. It fired.

Precaution #3: No matter how high on the beach you drag the dinghy, tie it to a tree.

Chapter 25
<u>Stay Tuned for the Following Message</u>

They wash up in many shapes and sizes. Some clear, some green, one even filled with sparkling bits of tinsel and confetti. If you think, like I used to, that messages in bottles were found only between the pages of Nicolas Sparks novels, stay tuned.

The first time I spotted a flash of white inside a clear bottle high up on the beach, it gave me the same fluttery feeling I used to get when hunting for arrowheads with my dad. In early spring, we'd spend Saturday afternoons tromping through fields near the Rock River in northern Illinois. Late afternoon light cast long shadows, highlighting bits of rock and, sometimes, the sharp tip of an arrowhead.

It's the same on the beach. You can walk one direction with your antennae fully raised and operational and spot nothing more than plastic hard hats and florescent light tubes. Turn around and light + luck + fate = treasure, but before you pack your bags for The Bahamas, it's almost never the monetary kind.

Japanese blown-glass fishing floats vie for first place salvage honors along with bottles containing messages. But since glass floats have been universally replaced by plastic, they're an increasingly rare find. Bottle messages, however, may actually be on the upswing with the rising popularity of cruise ships. We've found several messages written on cruise line letterhead with the pertinent information filled in on a prepared form: Date, location, name of ship, address to use if responding to the message.

No matter what their origin, though, I can't believe anyone tucks a message into a bottle and tosses it into the ocean without pausing to think, to reflect, to wonder. They must watch it bob away as the boat moves forward. They may consider the chances of anyone finding it, and if it's found, the chances the finder will respond. I love thinking about that moment in a stranger's life and how it magically resolves when I bend down to pick up their bottle, pry open the seal and read what they've written.

Last year Fritz found a message dropped from a sailboat on New Year's Eve, 1997, by a woman cruising with her family. He wrote to the address she'd included to tell her when and where the bottle had been found. It took her almost a year to reply; reading her letter we understood why. One of her children who'd been along on the sailing trip had since been involved in a life-threatening accident. This mother wrote about how much it meant to her to remember the night she'd thrown the bottle in the ocean, before her family changed in tragic and unanticipated ways. She wrote that it gave her hope for experiencing another New Year's Eve on the moonlit deck of a sailboat when her family was once again well and intact.

In December I'd found a bottle on the beach right in front of our house. "Greetings," the note began. Please write to:

Ricky Williams

P.O. Box 61107

Umatilla, Florida

"On the way to San Juan from Florida. Let me know when and where you found this bottle. Dropped @ approx - 25°N - 75°E. Thank You. Your Friend, Ricky."

Below the address was a penciled happy face with half a smile. It looked like a child had drawn it, though an adult hand printed the note. There was also a sticker affixed: a fierce eagle flying over an American flag. My best guess said it was a boy's voice, dictated to a parent. The happy face and the eagle were Ricky's additions. I wrote back with that in mind, telling Ricky it had been Esme who'd brought my attention to the bottle by first sniffing at it.

Outgoing mail either flies out on the twice-weekly BahamasAir flight or gets a trip on the mailboat. Even sending it airmail I figured it would take at least a month to arrive Stateside. When a neighbor handed me a thick packet—we take turns picking up the mail from the postmistress's office in Colonel Hill—in mid-January, I at first didn't recognize the return address. By the time I finished reading all the enclosed documents, it was clear my bottle-message reply experience would be a little different than Fritz's.

I'd been right about Ricky. He was a seven-year-old boy. This time his letter was in his own hand, a charmingly printed, crossed-out, reprinted note:

Dear Mari- Thank You for finding my bottle and writing back to me and thats why I'am writing back to you and your Dog Esme. by the way what kind of dog is Esme. One last sentence before - I'm am dog crazy And I'am GoinG to love to meet Esme And you someday.

Take care of Esme and Yourself, Ricky Williams

Also enclosed was a two-page letter from his father, Bill, written on, yup, New Year's Eve. (What is it about bottles, messages and New Year's Eve?) He thanked me for my letter to his son. Setting a new mail speed record, it had arrived on Christmas Eve.

Ricky's life was very "difficult," Bill wrote. "He is heavily medicated for ADHD plus ODD (society makes it that way)! Public school says they can't make me give it to him but he would not be able to attend [school] if he didn't [take it].

Paragraph three made me sit up a little straighter: "You sure are living my dreams for Ricky to be somewhere like Crooked Is., to be home schooled and live a drug free life without people who don't understand him. His own mother hasn't even contacted him in over 4 years, but that's another story!"

The accompanying photos showed Bill and Ricky aboard a cruise ship and at several Caribbean ports of call. One, taken in what looked like their cabin, was of Ricky holding a photo of a wide man in a striped shirt wielding a fishing rod. The letter explained: "[The cruise] was arranged by my cousin whose brother passed away last July and our trip was to cast his ashes in the Caribbean so when he travels with his own boat in the islands his brother's memory will travel with him. (You haven't seen Cousin Denny? His ashes were put in a bottle too by Ricky.)

Mercifully, while the two bottles may have been tossed together, Cousin Denny's ocean voyage took him to a different final resting place than Ricky's message.

I looked at the photos many times over the next weeks and finally replied to Ricky's letter. When fate, or bottles, throws people together, I figured sometimes you just have to play it out. But I never heard another word.

Chapter 26
<u>Big Sale, Save 100%, No Limit</u>

The hottest items in my sister Carla's Tinkertown Museum gift shop are the surprise grab bags. These $3 bestsellers, which are no more then a brown lunch bag filled with an assortment of closeout inventory, have the same allure as the twenty-six mile sandy shopping mall on Crooked Island. You just don't know what you'll find until you walk the beach. Not that you can't put in an order, but that's an advanced shopping technique I'll get to later.

Every day there are two high tides. That means the inventory has a chance to turn over *sixty* times a month! It's not unlike shopping in a megastore like Costco or Sam's Club; you can walk for miles looking for a specific item only to find it has been discontinued.

The sandy mall always has something on sale. What exactly it is depends on what shipping disasters have occurred on the North Atlantic the previous couple of years. According to dated messages found in bottles on the beach, it takes approximately two years for something to drift from the coast of France, Spain or Portugal to Crooked's north shore, less for anything in between. There is a greater selection on the shelf during the winter months, when blustery blows charge out of the north and churn the seas to a frenzy. Anything trapped in the Sargasso Sea or the barrier reefs busts loose and winds up on the beach.

Certain items are always in stock. Need rope, plastic containers, dimension lumber, shoes (rarely a pair), stainless steel fittings, buoys of any shape or size, furniture (rough), coconuts, ping pong balls, bamboo, wood or plastic crates, fish nets, oil drums, plastic or glass bottles? You've come to the right place. What items may lack in quality, color or style is made up for at checkout. Not only that, The Mall accepts returns but we usually take those to the dump.

Not long ago, The mall took delivery of several hundred heavy PVC artillery cartridge containers. They were about three feet long and looked like ornate, hexagonal fence posts. Local kids sold them for twenty-five cents each; they now line many island driveways.

A local musician and tavern owner found a two-foot tall teak carving of what appears to be an Asian imperial warlord who now presides over one end of the Double Deuce bar.

Last year, friends found a Navy drone, basically a guided missile used for target practice. They promptly dismantled it, salvaging all the avionics then displayed it in their yard. Shortly after, the sergeant stopped by to inform them of an obscure Bahamian law called "theft by finding." Translated, this means that anything washed up on a Bahamian beach belongs to the Bahamian government. A lot of speculation went into why Sarge was concerned about the drone, but he wanted it returned to the beach where it was found. A year later, the bits and pieces were still there.

What this means to all island residents is that we no longer beachcomb. We clean the beaches.

Mari and I use visualization to place specific orders. After we poured the columns for the front wall of the house, we needed a heavy header beam for the six-foot sliding glass door. No one had a 6"x10" piece of wood so I contemplated laminating something up from 2x10 stock. What we really wanted was a gnarly old timber to blend with the rock wall. We thought about that for a couple of weeks and one morning at the bottom of the steps to the beach lay our gnarly 6x10. It was about eight feet long with a few old iron bolts thrown in for a cosmetic touch. I trimmed off one worm-eaten end and it dropped into place.

We'd had a hard time crossing paths with Clinton, who besides being an electrician and fishing guide, sold soft drinks by the case. I went through a fair amount of Coke (imagine the Andrews Sisters singing "*Rum and Coca Cola*") and ginger ale, but had been out for some time. Before we found Clinton, a case of Pepsi washed ashore about a hundred yards from the house. The fact that it was Pepsi and not Coke only bothered me as far as checkout.

I thought a long rope would make a nice driveway border. One soon washed up at the bottom of our steps, but at 2½ inches in diameter, wasn't as thick as we wanted. However, when coiled into a cone, it made a splendid six-foot high entrance marker. A week later I found the driveway border, but it was several miles down the beach, accessible only by foot or dinghy. This required a major salvage operation—four hundred feet of five-inch diameter black hawser with two huge loops spliced into each end. With a neighbor's help, we snaked it down to the water where it weightlessly floated, then attached one end to the dinghy and hauled it two miles to a spot where the road met the beach. We coiled it into the back of the truck and drove home. With one end anchored at the entrance to the drive, we drove forward, laying it out as we went. A custom fit.

No matter what we need or desire, the mall provides. But its greatest attribute is the low-stress window-shopping with miles of soothing sand and surf Musak. It's a place that accommodates all levels of thought, from deep introspection to brainless flights of fancy, all without commercial interruption. Here you can find yourself or anything else that's washed up.

Chapter 27

<u>Locked Out</u>

On May 15th we fit boards into place to cover the house's ocean-facing glass door and windows. A layer of wood wouldn't do much to repel a direct hurricane hit, but it would offer some protection from anything less. The aluminum slatted jalousie windows we simply cranked shut. They were on their own. Crooked Island hadn't been ravaged by a major storm since Hurricane Donna in 1960. Forty years was a long time to stay lucky, but we were philosophical. If during hurricane season the Big Bad Wolf blew our house down, at least we wouldn't be in it.

We'd moved *San Diego* to the west side the previous day. It would be easier to leave at first light without having to tiptoe around the north shore's coral reefs. Early next morning, when Doug and Christel picked us up for the short trip to the beach where our dinghy waited, it felt for the first time like I was leaving home.

Anchored just behind us was a vessel that must have arrived during the night. *Starship*, a 175-ft. expedition yacht, was to San Diego as James Bond was to Inspector Clouseau. Her smallest tender was larger than our boat; a nimble helicopter perched like a hummingbird on an upper aft deck. Loading the last of our supplies on board *San Diego*, we could see crew in matching polo shirts scurrying from one cabin to another.

I turned the ignition key, the engine roared and Fritz hauled the anchor aboard. From shore, Doug and Christel waved and called goodbye. Poor *Starship*. Even on a multi-million dollar yacht in the middle of nowhere, you can still be disturbed at dawn by noisy neighbors.

This year the weather was with us. By the time we passed Chub Cay two days later, the Banks had flattened to glass. Esme and I sat on the bow for hours as we glided forward, suspended on invisible water above a continually unfolding panorama of ocean life, our own starship orbiting a crystal ball.

In Florida, a surprise waited. There's a lock on the Intercoastal Waterway near Stuart, fifteen miles from Indiantown, *San Diego's* summer home. After anchoring for the night in a public mooring area near one of Stuart's many bridges, we approached the lock early the next morning, already anticipating the end of the voyage, a hot shower (me) and a cold beer (Fritz). There didn't seem to the usual level of activity, which soon made perfect sense. The lock was closed for repair, and scheduled to stay closed for at least another week. The lockmaster's terse advice to us was to stay in the area. I got the feeling he'd been asked more than once about when it would reopen.

In four days, I had a flight leaving Orlando for New Mexico and a first anniversary surgery and oncology follow-up appointment. There were no alternate water-routes to the Indiantown Marina, but there was a park adjoining the lock. Lacking other alternatives, we parallel-parked along the waterway's bank, tethered San Diego to a sturdy tree and settled in to wait.

Esme, delighted at this turn of events, quickly wagged her way around what turned out to be a large community of semi-permanent park residents. They were mostly unemployed or underemployed single or divorced men who, with a Florida driver's license, could stay indefinitely in state parks for a nominal fee. In a northern environment they might have been in shelters or even homeless but Florida's weather made long-term tenting possible. They shared fish and useful tips with us, like the location of a one-dollar movie theater.

Next morning Fritz hitchhiked to the storage yard to retrieve our truck, and one blessed afternoon we stepped out of the already punishing Florida heat into the air-conditioned, buttered-popcorn heaven of *Crouching Tiger, Hidden Dragon*.

On the day of my flight we left for Orlando before dawn. After dropping me, Fritz returned to San Diego and was first in line several days later when the lock finally opened. He completed the voyage, emptied and cleaned the boat, had it hauled out of the water, moved it to the storage yard and was waiting with the truck when I walked out of Orlando's terminal five days later having been poked, prodded and declared well.

We drove north, temporarily trading everything Bahamian for everything Scandinavian. From conch fritters and Junkanoo to fish boils (a traditional cooking method, not a dermatological problem) and Scandinavian folk-dance festivals, our semi-annual cultural switch was less jarring than it may sound. But while to many summer residents Washington Island was a remote respite from big city life, to us it felt urban. Restaurants where we could order off a menu? A coffee house with an espresso machine? When a friend complained that Mann's Store had run out of arugula, all I could do was laugh.

We measured, cut and hammered our way through the next few months, which felt strangely familiar. When fall arrived and Esme refused to swim after the stick thrown in Lake Michigan, we knew it was time to find warmer water.

Chapter 28
Leave A Light On For Us

November, 2001. We are in the "Watermelon Capitol of the World" waiting for parts. Early yesterday, while cruising south on the interstate at 70 mph in our heavily loaded Ford, all five lug nuts sheared off the left rear wheel and it broke free. We slalomed between the concrete pillars of an overpass, sending up a rooster tail of sparks from the brake housing being ground off by pavement. I'll always remember Mari's sharp intake of breath and my frantic, delicate tap dance on the brake pedal and clutch before we scraped to a stop on the shoulder. Time-out here for a change of pants.

We managed to find the wheel hidden high on a hillside before I put my thumb out to hitch a ride for help. Minutes later, an official-looking SUV bristling with antenna pulled up. I used his phone to call for a tow and an hour later we were at the Ford dealership in Cordele, Georgia, hoping for an expeditious fix. Three days and six hundred dollars later we spit out the last of our watermelon seeds and rolled on down to Indiantown.

Early the next morning we retrieved the boat. By day's end we had the mildew scrubbed from the cabin and the boat's bottom reflected the sheen of a fresh coat of anti-fouling paint. Five days of shopping madness filled *San Diego's* hold as Esme slowly lost space to buckets of drywall compound, paint, lumber, furniture, beer and dry goods unavailable on Crooked Island. Our departure was preceded by the annual marina Halloween party, where costumes ranged from Cat Woman to walking armpits. The seedy Bubba element excelled with displays of paraphernalia from the local adult toy store. One guy strutted through the crowd wearing only a towel around his waist. Every time a woman walked near he pulled a string and a giant rubber penis popped out.

It wasn't hard to read Mari's look. It was time to shove off.

Blessed with little to no wind, we made an early morning break from Jupiter Inlet. We traversed a tame Gulf Stream directly to Nassau, dodging cruise ships out of Florida from midnight to dawn. After a brief overnight in Nassau we shot down the Exumas to Little Farmer's Cay.

While Esme and I explored the beach, Mari managed to hail a local restaurant. Later that evening there was a surprise birthday (my 52nd) dinner and cake waiting at the Ocean Cabin Restaurant. We were the only ones dining that night, over slices of cake we chatted with owners Earnestine and Terry Bains. Earnestine had a brother, she said, who'd spent time on Crooked Island working for a construction company. It was Martin, the reckless payloader driver who'd nearly totaled our truck. While we stumbled through a few "Oh's!" and "No Kidding's!" Earnestine shook her head and said, "We pray for him."

The sun rose on glassy seas, enticing us across Exuma Sound to the top end of Long Island. We tucked into Cape Santa Maria's crescent bay so Esme could run. The forecast out of Nassau called for increasing winds the next day. Our last sixty-mile leg would be in the open Atlantic, so after a quiet dinner aboard, we left for Crooked. After topping Long Island's northern tip, we cruised through the night down the island's windward side, exchanging only one radio call with a lumbering mailboat before picking up the 18-second flash from Bird Rock Lighthouse at 4 a.m.

Despite GPS navigation, nothing surpasses the comforting wink from an expected landfall. Made virtually redundant by today's electronic wizardry, lighthouses are packed so full of nostalgia that they'll only go out of existence when humans no longer read.

That being said, the Bird Rock light, a mile off Crooked's NW corner, is on the fast track to decrepitude. When we first visited Crooked, the lighthouse had been dysfunctional for several years. Local pressure and, I suspect, funding from cruise lines, convinced the government to send a Royal Bahamas Defense Force crew to the rescue. On the eve of the millennium the flash was back, bringing new life to Crooked's north shore with every sweep of the beacon. But like the sparkle in the eye of a centenarian, I wonder how long it can last.

Each year more flakes of rust fall from the cast iron spiral stairway. Gaping holes appear in the finely wrought treads and the once sturdy railing creates only an illusion of safety. The 112 ft. tower is a monument to exquisitely detailed British engineering and craftsmanship and will host generations of osprey nests to come. Solar cells, fresh batteries and a self-contained revolving light illuminate the night for now, but what happens when the stairway finally gives way and access for basic maintenance is gone?

The British recognized the need for a navigation light on Bird Rock in the mid-1800's. The reef-strewn entrance to the Crooked Island Passage had already claimed a good many hulls. The project began in 1866 with an estimated construction time of four years. Like so many major undertakings, estimates fell dramatically short. In this case the budget tripled and completion time stretched to ten years.

Materials for the finely tapered tower of hand-hewn limestone block came from the quarry at Gun Bluff, two miles east, then were barged across a coral-studded lagoon. Despite the barrier reef, the quarry landing was highly exposed to the northeast trade winds. Imported materials—everything but limestone—had to be first landed on Crooked then transferred to Bird Rock during periods of settled weather. Complicating the process was resistance from unenthusiastic Bahamian laborers who up until now had augmented their livelihood by salvaging cargo from ships wrecked on an unlit sea.

Like all remote lighthouses, infrastructure to support the keepers and their families was a major consideration. Water collection and storage, housing, cooking facilities, boat sheds and signal towers were all part of the design. The remaining woodwork and bronze fittings throughout still tell a story of loving attention to detail.

The light itself was a complex French-designed mechanism activated by counter-weights that hung down the center of the tower. A massive, triangular array of handcrafted prismatic lenses rotated freely in a tray of mercury and amplified the white light generated from a kerosene-fired mantle. The actual flash could be seen from the deck of a ship twenty miles out, the robust loom reached another thirty.

Hartman Scavella is one of Crooked's old-timers. A short bronze man with frosted, tightly coiled hair, Harty has two bad knees and a smile brighter than the Bird Rock light. He worked as a lightkeeper before the switch to electric lighting.

"We took four-hour shifts, but they didn't want us to sleep," he said. "They put a block on the weight cable so it only run the light for an hour at a time. When we saw the light slow down we run fast to the top, give the glass a shove, run back down and crank up the weight." He laughed. "They always knew if you been asleep."

If a passing ship noted a problem with the light, like being stalled or completely out, the observation was entered in the ship's log with time and date. The entry would eventually make its way to the British Lighthouse Commission, who in turn checked the Bird Rock staff schedule to see who had failed at their duties. Even in the remote, southeast Bahamas, Big Brother was watching.

Chapter 29
Pour, Paint, Rake, Scrape

When a project is no longer "under construction," is it then "above construction"? Or is it "over" construction? Whatever the semantics, when we arrived for our fourth season on Crooked Island it soon became clear that because we now had walls, roof, plumbing and electricity, Fritz was ready to declare the cottage at Lot 90 Seahorse Shores a wrap.

Not so fast, my dear.

While he gazed longingly at fish and lobster-rich coral heads, I sighed heavily whenever setting a plate on the still-plywood kitchen counters. He reached for his guitar; I reached for a paintbrush. He opened a book; I opened a can of "Cozy Melon" or "Sandstone" and began to stir. It was usually enough to redirect his attention, but occasionally even these finely honed passive-aggressive techniques failed. It was time to call for backup.

Jim Guthro lived a quarter-mile east of us in a flamingo-pink bungalow. Like Don and June McMillan, Jimmy G. had been coming to Crooked Island for thirty years. He was a retired Canadian Broadcasting Corporation executive and professional trumpet player who had better taste in music and books than hairpieces.

Jimmy loved our idea for pouring concrete counter-tops. Every time he dropped by for morning coffee or an evening cocktail, he wanted to know when, exactly, the project would start. Fritz tried his best to distract him, and truthfully, it wasn't hard. Years before, Jimmy had conceived and directed a weekly television news show. (When the format was later adopted in the U.S. by CBS it was, and still is, called *60 Minutes*.) Jimmy had so many stories about familiar people it became a game to name celebrities he hadn't interviewed.

"Dan Ackroyd? Of course I knew Dan Ackroyd. He had an act. He was funny. But he came in my office one day and he had a GIRL with him. LOSE the GIRL, I told him. Then I sent him down the hall to see Lorne Michaels."

Fritz's delay tactics worked for a while, but eventually he saw he was no match for the powerful combination of Jimmy's enthusiasm and my whining. We soon shaped a frame around the counter-top, then laid in a mat of wire in preparation for an on-site pour. Working with concrete allowed design flexibility, we created rounded corners and a flowing edge to mirror the ocean's undulation.

Using the bag of white cement we'd brought aboard *San Diego*, Fritz mixed coarse beach sand then added buff-colored dye until our committee of three agreed it was the right shade of peachy-tan. From the wheelbarrow it was bucketed to the kitchen and poured in the forms. Timing was crucial: the final troweling had to be precisely timed to result in a polished surface.

When the form was full, a half-bucket of mix remained. Jimmy suggested Fritz use what was leftover to make a bowl. The results, both counter and bowl, were such that I retrieved Fritz's spear from where I'd hidden it. He soon disappeared into the ocean. Jimmy and I high-fived.

It's eight in the evening in early January. The cool northeast trades rustle the silver palms surrounding the house; a mild surf washes the beach below. Mari and I are nodding off on the couch with a couple of gripping works of literary fiction when we hear a muffled voice over the VHF radio, "Sandog, Sandog, Pittstown here." I know the voice and it can only mean one thing. I feel a rush like from a double shot of espresso.

I key the mic. "Yeah Reggie, what's up?"

"Hey mon, we got music tonight. Can you make it?"

Reggie is Crooked Island's answer to Jimmy Buffett. Six slender feet and all arms and legs, he wears his hair close-shaved with three bead-adorned braids at the neck. He's the crowd pleaser, the dance floor motivator, vocal golden boy, rhythm guitar and undisputed leader of the band.

I play the harmonica, Crooked Island's answer to the horn section. About a dozen times a year the inn at Pittstown hosts a hoppin' crowd that demands "rake and scrape," a distinctive Bahamian fusion of calypso, rock and country that puts its own spin on boogie. Most settlements in the Islands have their own rake and scrape band ready to perform at the slightest hint of a party.

As the name implies, it's heavy on rhythm and light on melody. A screwdriver raked across the teeth of an old saw creates the distinctive zip of this musical genre. And nobody plays the saw quite like Reggie's wife, Rochelle. She tops Reggie by four inches and has a regal stature that conjures visions of African tribal matriarchs, not to mention a tireless right arm.

At twenty-something, Ronnie is the band's youngest member. He plays the drum, a single goat hide stretched across the end of a 55-gallon barrel. He wears a knit hat with long, floppy earflaps that cover a tightly cornrowed scalp. When he thumps out a rhythm on the drum, the flaps dance like a conductor's baton. Robbie, the charter captain and dive-master, plays a delicate lead on his Fender guitar and makes us a quintet.

Spontaneity is the essence of island time, so gig notification is rarely less than an hour in advance. I gather up the necessary cords, mic, amp, and harmonicas and already my head nods to the familiar beat. Mari can't decide if she'll attend or not.

"It's not about the music," she explains. "It's the guys who go from huggers to mouth kissers after a few drinks." I suggest a veil, which elicits rolled eyes. There is also another problem. No one ever asks Mari to dance. It seems the local men are too shy to ask her without my permission and I'm busy playing music. I offer to make a general announcement relinquishing dance rights, but she doesn't appear convinced. When I add that if we go early the huggers will still be huggers, she agrees.

The music won't start until at least 9:30 but I go early to tune the guitars to my harmonica. If I arrive late I'll have to make do— once the band fires up there's no turning back. After all, what's a volume control knob for if not to override minor discrepancies in pitch?

We drive the mile to the inn on a moonlit marl road, headlights optional. Diners have pushed back their chairs and Reggie is still tending bar. "Flamboyant" perfectly describes his mood and I surmise the guests have bought him a few rounds of his favorite high-test Puerto Rican rum. Now it's imperative I personally tune his guitar. I've learned from experience that his concern about

181

proper pitch decreases as the amount of rum increases. (On the up side, he'll be in rare form as the front man.)

Most people come here to fish, and the walls in the bar are a testament to the angler's guile. In the crowd, we're surrounded by snippets of fish lore, "Smoked five-hundred yards off the reel with full drag...Damn sharks took all but the head...Did a lot of fishin' but no catchin'...Landed a sixty pound wahoo."

Rochelle and Ronnie are already there. Robbie pops in around nine but it takes him twenty minutes to make his way through all the fishermen who want his advice. Reggie's mic stand has disappeared so we hang the mic from an overhead light shade.

We're crowded into one end of the narrow barroom, blocking the entrance to both bathrooms. Traffic is shunted through the kitchen. Reggie, finally free, straps on his guitar and steps up to the mic: "Ladies and gentlemen, fasten your seat belts and prepare for blastoff!"

This is where Reggie deviates from the guitar norm. Rather than strum, he bangs flat-handed across the strings, effectively turning his guitar into a percussion instrument. (Didn't I say we were strong on rhythm?) No one in the band knows what song he'll open with but everything we play is in the key of "C" or "G" and they all start the same.

We squeeze almost ten minutes out of *The Sloop John B* turned turbo-diesel. Dancer's elbows threaten the band. A drunken fisherman reaches for one of my harmonicas. I slap his hand away and he reacts as if bitten. (Sorry, but that's like lending your toothbrush to a stranger.) We follow *Sloop* with *Bang Bang Lulu* and *Doctor, Doctor I Got The Flu*. Same three chords, the chic-chicka-chic of the saw never falters and Reggie is into serious guitar abuse.

Our breaks are regulated by the tension on the goatskin drumhead. When Ronnie can't make it ring, we stop and send the drum to the kitchen to "give it fire." This is done by passing the head over all four stove-burners set on high. Once heated, the skin tightens and we can roar for another forty minutes.

Our repertoire is relative to the volume of alcohol consumed. Rum may relax Reggie's tuning standards but it stimulates his memory. I feel left out by the end of the night—drinking anything but water makes me burp, not a good attribute for a harmonica player.

Reggie turns the third set into a Jimmy Buffet medley, which, apart from the words, sounds a lot like the Phil Stubbs medley he earlier performed. The dance floor is oblivious. A dozen or more locals have drifted in and I've spotted Mari in the dance crowd. I guess she's convinced her partners that's she's free to make her own choices.

There is no last call for closing, the band just bops till it drops, which can be as late as 3 a.m., then everyone staggers home. Mari and I take advantage of the moonlight and strip for a midnight plunge to wash off the lounge cologne. We laugh over the lyrics of the last song and agree: one of the best things about rake and scrape is that it doesn't happen every night.

Woe is me
Shame and scandal in the family
Woe is me
Shame and scandal in the family
Once there was a family
With much confusion as you will see
It was a mama and a papa and a boy who was grown

Plunge

He wanted to marry, have a wife of his own
Found a young girl that suited him nice
Went to his papa to ask his advice
His papa said: "Son, I have to say no,
This girl is your sister, but your mama don't know."

Chapter 30
Excerpt: Crooked Island Diary

Wednesday, January 23

Two planes crashed at Pittstown today, one right after the other. Both pilots are flight instructors but don't know each other. Both flew Cessna 310's, a rather old and rare model. Both came in too low, hit the sand berm at the end of the runway, then crashed. One was much worse than the other. Nobody hurt, but the pilot of the total wreck is a total wreck. After hours of weeping on Tammy's shoulder, she locked him out of her room so she could get some sleep. No one remembered to turn off the automatic emergency beacon on one of the planes, so at 1am a Coast Guard helicopter flew in and woke everyone up all over again.

Saturday, 26th

Insult to injury, the pilot of the total wreck crawled through the bush to take photos of what was left of his plane and got a nasty case of poisonwood. His right arm and back now closely resemble raw hamburger (that itches) with blisters.

Friday, February 1

A team from an air salvage company arrived to dismantle the planes and prepare the parts for transport back to the States, via mail boat. They expect to be here for at least a week.

Thursday, 7th: 7 a.m.

We loaded eight people and a trailer full of supplies onboard *San Diego* for an overnight excursion to Castle Rock, site of the beautiful old lighthouse that is sister to Bird Rock's. An hour into the trip it starts to rain. Two hours into the trip the waves start climbing. Everyone eats oatmeal cookies. We catch only one tiny tuna on the way, and revise our cookout plans to feature chicken.

11 a.m.

A 100-foot Bahamian Defense cutter hails us, wanting to know what we're up to in these waters. Captain Fritz explained we're on our way to Castle Rock to camp and sightsee. They all looked confused, then one of them said, "Well, have a good time" and the boat pulled away.

1 p.m.

Arrived Castle Rock. The lighthouse is magnificent. It's a few feet taller (115' total) than Bird Rock, and made of limestone. It's been recently repainted by a government team and from thirty feet looks great. Close up, we see they've gone crazy with the paint sprayer, covering not only solid surfaces but also windows, solar panels, batteries and surrounding foliage. The empty paint cans have been thrown in the bush. I surprised an owl that made a nest in the wall of a crumbling outbuilding. The wreck of Haitian freighter rusts in the bay; the top of the cabin is now an osprey nest.

Sunset

Four skiffs roared into the bay with several men in each vessel. They looked as surprised to see us as we were to see them. They buzzed around in circles for a few minutes, then one boat headed toward our camp while another landed its crew down the beach. That group ran off into the bush. The other boat kept coming our way until Esme and Dude, Tammy's ancient yellow lab, barked a warning. From a safe distance, one guy called to us, wanting to know what we were doing there.

"Came to take pictures of the lighthouse," Christopher yelled back.

They looked us over—three guys, five women (two of them silver-haired)—and must have decided we were no threat.

"Doing some fishing tonight," the guy said. "But we'll be on the other side of the island. Have a good time." And off he went. Down the beach, the guys who'd disappeared into the bush returned, climbed aboard their boat and joined the rest of the flotilla.

None of us had ever seen fishermen dressed in polo shirts and slacks before, but we weren't asking questions. Nice to have the dogs along.

9 p.m.

We ate, then sang around the campfire accompanied by Fritz and Doug's guitars before retreating to the boat. Somehow, we left behind the poles for the tent Connie and June are sharing, so a coconut palm trunk is holding it up. The rain held off all evening and there was a dazzling show of stars. Later the clouds rolled back in, this time accompanied by wind. Half asleep in the cabin, Fritz and I felt the boat start to pitch and roll. He listened for a long time and then said, "I don't like the sound of this."

Friday, 8th, 7 a.m.

Wind: 25 knots with gusts to 30. Black storm clouds on the horizon. Captain's Orders: "Pack up fast, we're outta here."

10 a.m.

Big rollers with a nasty chop on top. Everyone is completely drenched but still singing and eating cookies. Christel dragged a line and caught a tuna. Chris improvised a raincoat from a garbage bag and hung off the cabin's roof rail to avoid getting seasick. June and Connie shared a thermos of coffee and compared notes about what a good time they were having. Tammy found a dry cubby up forward and snuggled in with Dude and a book. Doug hung in with Fritz at the helm. I huddled with Esme on the engine cover, thinking we couldn't have picked seven better people to share a less-than-perfect voyage.

2 p.m.

We radio Don when we're fifteen minutes from the village jetty and he tells us Crooked's weather has been horrible since the moment we left. He pretends he hasn't been worried.

Monday, 11th

Pittstown's owner and the air salvage company chief have an altercation on the runway about some piece of previous business gone bad. It ends in a shoving match and the salvage guy files assault charges with Sarge in Colonel Hill.

Tuesday, 12th

The air salvage chief agrees to drop charges if Pittstown's owner will allow the salvaged plane parts to be taken off his property.

Wednesday, 13th

We pass a flatbed on the road loaded with wings, tails and props.

Friday, 15th—Wednesday, 20th

Rain. Wind. Mosquitoes. Window-trim painting. Garden blew away for second time.

Monday, 25th

Connie came over to tell us her name reached the top of the list for a spot in a retirement center in Santa Barbara, California. A casita will be open and waiting in May. As much as she loves Crooked Island, she told us, there's just not enough going on here for her. While she'll continue to visit every year, Connie-Mom, at 78, has decided to dive back into the mainstream.

Chapter 31
<u>Blackbirds at Midnight</u>

WHUP! WHUP! WHUP! WHUP! WHUP! WHUP! WHUP! WHUP! WHUP!

Rattled awake from sound sleep, Mari and I groaned. The house shook with each spin of the blades. Esme's nose was already pressed to the door, hackles up. I peered into the darkness. A shadow, deeper than the night sky, flitted by a hundred feet from where I stood. I tumbled back into bed. "Our tax dollars at work. I wonder if they think they're being stealthy without the lights."

It was the third time in a week the DEA Blackhawk helicopter had buzzed the north shore at midnight. It wasn't that unusual, but generally at least a week went by between late night visits. We figured they must have gotten wind of an impending drug drop, prompting the stepped-up patrol.

At least the U.S. Coast Guard made their passes during the day when we were awake and could wave. But even though a uniformed body always sat in the open hatch, legs dangling, camera poised, no one ever waved back. (We'd love to have a copy of those photos documenting four years of construction. We could make a time-lapsed slide show and watch our house bloom like a flower.)

Helicopter traffic did seem to increase when certain individuals were in residence. Curious as we might have been, we chose to remain steadfastly ignorant of any underground economics fueling

Crooked Island. It was hard not to notice, though, the lack of tourism and other commerce relative to the volume of new cars and trucks, boats, televisions and appliances that rolled off the mailboat each week.

When Landrail Point's primary school was converted into a library, a grand opening was held. My sister Carla and her friend Eric, who was visiting for the first time, attended the party and overheard some kids discussing an out-island version of winning the lottery. It began: "When I get my suitcase full of money..."

A quick tour of Bahamian history is enlightening: After the disappointing results of the Revolutionary War, England divvied up The Bahamas among Loyalists seeking to escape retribution in the new, unfriendly, USA. These were wealthy Southern plantation owners who, when relocating to the islands, brought their families, their slaves and in some cases, their dismantled mansions. When all forms of commercial agriculture ultimately failed, the landowners bailed, leaving the Bahamian out-islands to the now freed slaves. As anyone in their situation would, they did whatever was necessary to survive.

Looting shipwrecks, or "wrecking"—deliberately luring a ship off course by rigging a false light—was all part of the game. Gunrunning during the Civil War created the first bull market, followed by rum-running during U.S. Prohibition. In a society with piratical roots, is it any wonder some of the newest generation might carry on the tradition of handling the latest high-profit merchandise?

Lots of stories make the rounds: Plane crashes with huge amounts of cash recovered. New homes suddenly built on choice pieces of property. Spectacular beach finds having nothing to do with shells. Local residents suddenly hauled off to Nassau.

One morning we woke to find a squad of camo-clad soldiers walking the beach in front of our house. They'd camped overnight in a nearby lot and were searching the area for missing contraband. We weren't too sure what "contraband" looked like, but for the next several weeks had fun talking about what we'd do if we found a suitcase full of money.

Chapter 32
Goodbye, John

"Thank the Lord for life," John Scavella used to say when Fritz or I asked how he was doing. Even when we knew things weren't going so well and even later, when he was dying.

John was the proprietor of John Scavella's Grocery Shop, a small shack behind his house at the end of a rocky, pitted path. Driving it was adventure enough to make the half-hour trip from Landrail Point worthwhile even on the rare occasions that John or his wife Mary weren't home. But it was because of the rocks, and the marl-enriched soil beneath them, that John's garden yielded the bounty it did. It was because of John that nobody really minded his driveway.

John was a small man, brown and bent, blind in one eye. He laughed an old man's wise laugh. His warmth was the same temperature for those he knew well and those he didn't.

John's VHF radio handle was "One Dollar," so christened for his legendary fund-raising prowess during island community auctions. As with the format for Connie's puppet show, Crooked Islanders collected impressive sums of money for special projects by organizing programs of songs and skits then bidding on them, one dollar at a time. What relative could resist parting with a dollar (or more) after listening to a three-year-old's version of "Jesus Loves Me?" One Dollar Scavella knew exactly who to tap and how hard.

We didn't visit John to patronize his grocery shop, though he stocked a few basic items and sometimes even pint-sized tubs of Dairy Maid ice cream, complete with plastic spoons. We went to John's to bask in his company and pick his citrus.

The first time we stopped, he listened politely to our house-building stories, which at that time involved much sand shoveling, rock moving and cement mixing. I think I had the notion that John, a hard-working man, would take more kindly to us once he knew we weren't afraid to sweat. But he just laughed and said, "Take it from a one-eyed man. Life too short to work all the time. You got to enjoy yourself, too. Don't you forget that."

On that visit, we first convened under the grapefruit tree. John produced a long pole with a basket attached to one end, handed it to Fritz, then squinted up into the branches. When John spotted one he liked, he pointed until Fritz cupped it in the basket, gave it a shake and brought it down, his hands collecting a dozen nasty slivers from the pole in the process. This was repeated from tree to tree until Fritz, trying not to grimace, had harvested a dozen grapefruits, tangerines and oranges.

John wouldn't let us pay him that first day. He was happy to know us, he said, and hoped we'd come back to see him. We did, but not nearly enough. Two years later John got sick with stomach cancer. He and Mary, who is nearly deaf and physically frail, continued to make do on their own, but as the months passed it was obvious to their close friends that he was failing, and in pain. I wish I could say that John had the best medical care, the most advanced treatment available. He didn't. But he had people who loved him and respected his wish to die at home and not "poked full of holes" in a Nassau hospital.

John couldn't get out of bed the last month of his life. Friends installed a washing machine for Mary when they realized she was washing sheets by hand, every day. They scrounged pain pills for John near the end. People from every tiny settlement in every corner of the island came to bring soup or fish or hold his hand. You could hope to die with less pain than John, but it would be hard to die with more love. And near impossible to top his funeral.

Fairfield's church sits on a modest slope just off a paved road, a stone's throw from John Scavella's Grocery Shop. Although I knew regular worship services were still conducted there, I had never seen it with its somber brown doors and shuttered windows thrown open. It seems larger than most Crooked Island churches due to its twin-peaked roofs that form an "M," as if two smaller churches slid together.

Inside, hand-hewn timber beams crisscross the ceilings. Walls are a foot thick, painted white and adorned with velvet paintings of Christ, the Last Supper and angels in floating attitudes. Wooden pews, pulpit and altar are handmade. It is a living space, still connected to the hands and hearts that built it.

Fritz and I arrived fifteen minutes early for the funeral. Even then, every row of pews, except those in front reserved for John's family, was full of people. The Bahamian custom of starting events at least an hour after the announced time clearly didn't apply to funerals. At least not this one. An usher handed us a program and pointed to a few empty seats next to the choir entrance, which to me looked uncomfortably close to where the island elders and ministers were starting to assemble: Mission Control for the entire service.

I was sure that except for babes in arms, we two Americans had known John for less time than anyone else in that crowded church.

I wasn't about to plop myself down facing three hundred bereaved friends and relatives as if angling to sing a solo. We were there to pay our respects, not intrude. I suddenly felt very white and out of place. Not to mention underdressed.

Funeral fashion protocol is black, white or a combination of both. Hats, too. I had the colors right, but in my plain cotton shirt and Eddie Bauer skirt I could have faded right out of existence amidst the glow and shimmer of lace, organza, crinoline and emotion.

Latecomers continued to arrive and as the empty seats around us disappeared so did my apprehension, even though the next three hours weren't remotely like any funeral I had ever attended. Lutherans do not say goodbye this way.

John's body lay in a wooden coffin assembled by the members of the Burial Society. The lid was closed, but a viewing window framed his face. Crooked Island has no embalming facility. Bodies are kept frozen—there is a locker especially for this purpose—until burial in one of the many village graveyards that dot the island. Did I mention John's funeral was three hours long on a hot, still May afternoon? Did I mention the church at Fairfield has no air-conditioning? I thought of John and why he always provided spoons with the ice cream he sold.

The family began to enter the church. Nephews, nieces, cousins, then Mary, supported by her daughter and young grandson. Mary, a tiny woman, grew large in grief. She stumbled down the aisle to the casket and threw herself across the lid. Her keening was in some private soul-language, unfiltered, free of self-consciousness. And it was loud. It soared. Her whole body shook and rattled.

All the while cameras flashed. At least two tape recorders caught every moan, every lamentation. Fritz and I locked eyes after watching a video-cam operator do a slow pan across the casket's viewing window.

Once Mary was pulled off the coffin and helped to her seat, the service began. Master of Ceremonies was Mr. Linkwood Ferguson, more commonly known as "Dispatch." From his hilltop home in the center of the island he uses his VHF radio to relay messages, make public announcements and generally keep abreast of what's happening at all times. He is also the minister of St. Paul's Baptist Church of Cabbage Hill and, as we were about to find out, runs a tidy funeral.

There were at least a dozen men seated behind the podium where Dispatch stood, all waiting to speak on behalf of their departed friend and brother. Most looked extremely old, another reason to move things along. Dispatch introduced the first speaker, then looked him in the eye and said, "You got two minutes."

When time allowed had expired, John Thompson strummed a single chord on his guitar; his sister Dorcas echoed it on piano, followed by his son Dennis on drums. Hymns were interspersed between speakers and while the words were of losses to be endured and storms to be ridden out, the trio of musicians laid down such a sexy jazz-fusion interpretation it sounded more like gospel in a piano bar. It was an effort to not get up and dance.

For the first hour, except for outbursts of weeping, the funeral rocked and rolled politely along. Then John's niece came forward and all heaven broke loose.

Wails and thumps issued forth from a convulsing knot of people under a velvet painting of the Lord's Supper, about mid-sanctuary. I couldn't see what the commotion was at first, so like everyone else, I stood. Ushers were on either side of a handsome, stout young woman who seemed to be making her way to the front of the church. Every few steps she collapsed (the thumps) and the rest of the family reacted (the wails).

When she made it to the steps that led to the podium, it was as if whatever possessed her wouldn't wait any longer. She opened her mouth and started to sing but it wasn't like anything I'd ever heard. Every note was stripped clean to its essence, a direct line to grief. It was pure, powerful and a little frightening, like someone singing in tongues. The hair stood on my arms. With each verse Niece Scavella upped the emotional ante. By the time she was carried back to her seat, John's funeral had taken its gloves off. It was time for the Nephew.

He had been sitting so quietly among the older men, I'd forgotten he was there. When Dispatch introduced him as John's nephew from Nassau, I expected another mini-eulogy. We were two hours into the service and the seats were hard. There was no breeze from the open door behind us. Mourners had turned programs into fans. The hot emotional charge that ricocheted around the church fueled my concern regarding premature thaw.

Nephew Scavella took the stand and somehow we knew that John's funeral wasn't over yet. He began quietly enough. He spoke of his uncle's virtue and of his value to his people, his church and his world. Then the picture got bigger. Admonitions replaced lamentations and after each one John's nephew shouted, "CAN I HAVE A WITNESS?" And the crowd of mourners hollered back, "AMEN."

For the next forty-five minutes we were in professional hands.
"LET'S SAY AMEN!"
His topics were varied, his repertoire vast.
"AMEN!"

No sin was too small to escape mention.

"LET'S SAY HALLELUJAH!"

He marched up and down the aisles of the sanctuary.

"HALLELUJAH!"

He stood over John in his coffin and shouted into the window.

"CAN I HAVE A WITNESS?"

He shook his fists against the world of sin, a human firecracker with a lit fuse ready to take us all with him when he blew.

"LET'S SAY AMEN!"

Then John Thompson winked at me, plucked a few notes and the Nephew took his seat. (HALLELUJAH!) A sigh rose from the congregation as they retrieved hymnals and sang a final song. Pallbearers assembled to carry the coffin from the church. We quietly slipped away then, feeling the next part of the ceremony was more appropriate for family and closest friends.

It's a short trip to the cemetery by the beach where John Scavella would be laid to rest, a cup and plate placed on the mound of sand to make sure he wouldn't be hungry on his journey to heaven. I hoped they'd add a grapefruit.

Chapter 33
<u>An Uncommon Life</u>

We're standing at the bottom of the stairs leading to the beach, but it's gone. The sea washes over a jumble of angular white rock that, until today, had been covered with three feet of sugary sand.

Every time a cold front blows through from the northwest the tides and current conspire to consume the beach. But at the same time we're presented with a new opportunity. This time at low tide, we scramble for the flat rocks and haul them to the bluff. Soon we'll have enough to build a stone wall in front of the patio.

As the front passes, the wind shifts to the east. Six to eight inches per day, the beach slowly returns until it reaches our bottom step. Each day the shoreline morphs into a new invitation to walk, run or swim.

It's this variety in our lives that keeps synapses firing, boredom non-existent and pleasure in the now. The ripples from the plunge we took in 1997 seem to build and recede with the same consistency as the beach. As we build relationship and self-awareness, the past recedes, and we're once again at the whim of our own choices.

In the Bahamas, when you arrive somewhere, you've reached. "When did you reach?" we're asked when we return each fall to Crooked Island. We report our most recent arrival, but really, it was a reach long ago that landed us here.

Ours is only one story. We don't always want, or have the opportunity to change the world around us, working instead with our inner landscape to alter perception, attitude, perspective. But there are times when changing the world around us changes the world within, revealing paths that were not before visible.

A friend recently finished hacking a trail to the ocean that bypasses a rocky bluff, making it possible to hike to a cove where turtles love to play.

"The entrance is a little hidden," he said. "Look for a bit of green net hanging and you'll know you've found it. The trail is rough, but you'll be able to follow it. When you get to a natural opening, you'll see some flat rocks. Look for the palm tree on the other side and you'll know you're on the right path. Keep going 'til you reach the beach. There's a little rise above the water but it's a deep and sandy bottom, so when you get there you can just—"

"We know," I said, and smiled at Fritz. "Plunge."

<u>Afterword</u>

Thank you for taking this journey with us. The adventure continues as we now look forward to our 18th season on Crooked Island. Don't forget to look for more photos, stories, recipes, you name it, on our website and Facebook author pages:

www.plungethebook.com
www.facebook.com/marichristineanderson
www.facebook.com/pages/Fritz-Damler/388247417952821?ref=hl

We'd love to hear your stories, too, about crafting and living an uncommon life, whether you're at midlife, beyond, or not even close.

All the best,
Mari & Fritz